For Orange and the States

The Army of the Dutch Republic, 1713–1772

Part II: Cavalry and Specialist Troops

Marc Geerdink-Schaftenaar

Helion & Company

Helion & Company Limited
Unit 8 Amherst Business Centre
Budbrooke Road
Warwick
CV34 5WE
England
Tel. 01926 499 619
Fax 0121 711 4075
Email: info@helion.co.uk
Website: www.helion.co.uk
Twitter: @helionbooks
Visit our blog http://blog.helion.co.uk/

Published by Helion & Company 2018
Designed and typeset by Mach 3 Solutions Ltd (www.mach3solutions.co.uk)
Cover designed by Paul Hewitt, Battlefield Design (www.battlefield-design.co.uk)
Printed by Henry Ling Limited, Dorchester

ISBN 978-1-911628-13-2

British Library Cataloguing-in-Publication Data.
A catalogue record for this book is available from the British Library.

Contents

Introduction

This book is the second of two volumes on the army of the Dutch Republic in the 18th century. Part I focussed on the uniforms and organisation of the infantry, which comprised the vast bulk of the army; this part is about the cavalry, artillery and specialist troops. Part I also contained a description of the Dutch Republic, its politics and organisation, and its involvement in the War of the Austrian Succession, ending with the Battle of Rocoux (11 October 1746). This part continues that description, starting with the campaign of 1747.

Added to this book are also appendices with additional information, such as a glossary of Dutch military terms.

Given the warm welcome Part I received, it has served its purpose, as I had intended: to make available information of the Dutch Army of the 18th century to an audience outside the Netherlands: and Part II will continue doing so.

There is nothing much I could add further, having said practically everything in my introduction in Part I. So in conclusion, I would like to thank the following:

First and foremost, the people at Helion and Company Publishing, for giving me the opportunity to publish these books, and for their patience; the people at the Rijksmuseum, Amsterdam, for their more than gracious permission to use their material, and their cooperation; Mrs. M. van Heek and the Stichting Edwina van Heek; Mr C. Baron van Kretschmar; Mr. C. Kuijpers, for providing me with information from his own research; Mr. M. de Leeuw of the Groninger Museum; Mr. N. Count Van Rechteren and the people at the Stichting Familie Van Rechteren Limpurg; Mr. P. Vesters of the Utrechts Landschap/Stichting Kasteel Loenersloot; and Mr. R. Vaara of the Armemuseum, Stockholm.

Marc Geerdink-Schaftenaar, October 2018

1

For Orange and the States

Memoirs of an Old Campaigner

In 2007, a translation was published of the memoirs of one Casimir Abraham Count von Schlippenbach, an officer in the States' Army who had fought in the War of the Spanish Succession and the War of the Austrian Succession. The 550-page manuscript, with the title *Journal de Ma Vie*, is kept in the National Archives in The Hague. Although the work is not unfamiliar, it had never been transcribed, translated and published before because of the many vivid descriptions of Schlippenbach's erotic encounters: the memoirs reveal the author to be quite a womaniser. The editors of *Het Staatse Leger* were disappointed that he wrote more about his affairs than about his military experiences. Nevertheless, it gives a vivid description of the officer corps of the States' army.

Schlippenbach was an officer of noble birth. He was born 12 April 1680 in Almahlen, Courland (present day Latvia), as the son of Christoph III Count von Schlippenbach, who became *inhaber* of a regiment of dragoons and rose through the ranks to major general. Other contemporary members of the Schlippenbach family were Major General Wolmar Anton Count von Schlippenbach, the former governor-general of Swedish Estonia and general in the Russian army; and Prussian cavalry commander Karl Friedrich Count von Schlippenbach. Casimir followed in his fathers' footsteps, and became a major, and later lieutenant colonel, in his father's regiment. They both fought in Spain during the War of the Spanish Succession; Casimir was wounded in the battle of Villaviciosa (10 December 1710), which led to the amputation of his right arm. As soon as he had recovered, he taught himself to ride and fight with one arm, practicing with the sabre and pistol left handed. It is an illustration of the zeal and loyalty of this cavalry officer, who worked tirelessly to keep up the standards of the regiment in which he served. After his father died in 1713 the regiment was almost disbanded, had he not offered to have the regiment sent to Britain 1715. He was surpassed by an infantry officer as colonel-proprietor of the regiment and would only achieve that rank in 1737, despite the rule that commissions were given based on seniority (in the 10 years before that, he had already been surpassed by 14 other officers for several promotions and commissions in the cavalry alone, some of whom had been mere *ritmeesters* or even 2nd lieutenants when he was already a lieutenant colonel).

Many officers were members of the ruling class, the *Regenten* [Regents], influential wealthy families with high positions in politics and the military. To them, a commission was above all a steady form of income, often sold to the highest bidder, and since all officers' positions were ratified by the Council of State, it paid off to have friends in high places. The crippling effects of this widespread corruption were visible at the manoeuvres at Oosterhout in 1732: it was clear that the rank and file were trained and ready, even though there was hardly a veteran in their midst; but the officer corps was severely lacking. More than once, Schlippenbach had to deal with incompetence and even insubordination from some of his officers. In his memoirs, he illustrates several of these incidents, such as with one of his captains in 1738:

> This little fop came to me one day, to ask me to ratify the promotion of someone in his company to quartermaster. This quartermaster had served previously as a dragoon in my company, and I had discharged him two years ago. He did not deserve to be promoted while the captain had more able men in his company [...]. But the captain persisted, despite the fact that the rank of quartermaster had been abolished. [...] Instead of listening to my good advice, he had the audacity to turn to the Council of State with an appeal in which he complained about the refusal on my part. I explained my decision with firm justifications, and the captain was then told he had to adhere to my command.

Several days after that, said captain refused to salute him properly on two occasions, but after being threatened with arrest, he apologised. That was not all: Schlippenbach wrote that his regiment never before had any worse officers than at that time: he had only two good captains; his lieutenant colonel, Baron Jekermans, was 'a drunk, a beast and a numskull, who had to be forced through court to do his duty'; and his major, Van Nes, he described as 'a nuisance, a slob, a madman and an idiot'. However, when Schlippenbach wanted them removed or at least reprimanded, the officers in question would write a letter of complaint to the Council of State, and in the end keep their positions. This was even the case when the regiment was to join the allied army in Germany in 1743:

> According to the orders of the States General, three squadrons of the regiment would have to march out, selected from the best men. Those officers not able to serve as such due to ill health, had to stay behind as well. I was therefore compelled to pass over two captains (Ingera and Coomans). One was struck with gout, and had to walk with crutches, the other had dropsy. But these two near-corpses complained by appeal to the Council of State that I had passed them over and demanded an explanation. I answered that it was because of their ill health, and said that they wouldn't even last four days of marching. Nevertheless, I was obliged to take them with me. But a worse fate befell these two captains, because after four days of marching, they had to stay behind. Because they wanted to follow the troops by coach from Cologne, one died there on the spot, and the other returned to the Republic.

During the campaign, it became painfully clear that the officers and men were unfamiliar with the necessities of campaign life, such as sending out sentries, performing watch duties and taking up advanced positions. Horses left standing near trees were getting sick from eating bark and leaves. The long marches through rugged terrain took their toll on the inexperienced men. The officers were in need of training, and the campaigns of 1743 and 1744, although unsuccessful, were used by the older officers as a refresher course, whilst the younger officers were getting some hands-on experience.

The battle of Fontenoy had been a disaster for the Dutch, as illustrated by the conduct of Colonel Matthias Hayko Appius, commander of the Hesse-Homburg Cavalry Regiment. Appius had panicked, turned and fled after the first shots, as did the whole regiment. Schlippenbach, the brigade commander, was now left with three squadrons. He kept his position on the left of the Hanoverian cavalry, despite being fired at from the French positions at Fontenoy. Seeing the column of British and Hanoverian infantry advance and break through the French lines, he was frustrated that there came no support from the Allied left flank. In the end, the column was forced to retreat, and the cavalry, having done little, followed. Schlippenbach was ordered to cover the retreat of the Dutch infantry, which he did successfully, and with very little losses. Colonel Appius had meanwhile written a panicked letter to the Council of State, saying that 'the entire United Army was destroyed', and that 'the woeful remnants of several regiments, without tents or baggage, which were plundered by French Hussars, had arrived in Ath'. During an interrogation into the affair, he admitted that his letter was a gross exaggeration and an outright fabrication. He was sentenced in a court martial to beg the military court and the Council of State for forgiveness, and to openly destroy his letter. Furthermore, he was declared wholly unfit to serve the Republic and removed from his positions. Major Sikkinga, two lieutenants, and a cornet of the regiment received the same sentence. Appius lived the rest of his life in Groningen, under the protection of the States of Stad en Lande. He wrote a pamphlet in his defence, stating that he rallied his wavering troops twice before they finally turned and fled, but he was forced to publicly recall that document, and copies of it were burned by the hangman in The Hague.

The reputation of the Dutch army had taken a severe blow. The following year, which again saw another string of French successes, the French were met in the field at Rocoux. Marshal Maurice de Saxe directed his attack against the Dutch forces on the left flank. But the States' army had learned its lesson, and although the Pragmatic Army had to give way and retreated towards Maastricht, it had not been the easy victory the French had hoped for. The bias against the Dutch troops was illustrated by Johannes van der Heij, an eyewitness of the battle:

> After the States' infantry had left the battlefield in a very good order, and [...] retreated towards Maastricht, the Imperial Cuirassier Regiment of Prince Birkenfeld [Count Palatine Wilhelm von Birkenfeld-Gelnhausen (1701–1760)] ran past me in great disarray: shortly after that, the Prince, who was a Lieutenant General for the Emperor and the States, and had an Imperial Regiment of

> Cuirassiers and a States' Cavalry Regiment under his command, [...] came by on horse equally as fast, shouting: 'Hold! you damned Dutchmen, hold!' [...] I told the commander: 'Your Grace is mistaken, those are not Dutchmen that are fleeing, those are Your Highnesses' Imperial Cuirassiers'. To which the Prince answered me: 'I thought these were my Dutch Birkenfelders'. Both Birkenfeld regiments were dressed the same, in white broadcloth coats, with pewer buttons, red facings and white lace around the hats; thus they looked the same, except for the cuirasses of the Imperial troops. [...] Similarly, Colonel Lewis, commanding the English Artillery, seeing the Utrecht Regiment of Foot Van Dorth perform miracles of heroism with amazing bravery, said to me: 'See those fine Hanoverians fight with bravery!', and when I told him: 'Forgive me, those are not Hanoverians, that is a Dutch Battalion', he answered me: 'That is impossible. Where have you ever seen Dutchmen fight like those brave men do?' He thought these fine men were Hanoverians, because at the time, the battalion was still dressed in red clothing with yellowish facings.

Schlippenbach in his memoirs gives credit to *Ritmeester* De Rivecourt of Birkenfeld's Regiment:

> That regiment [Birkenfelds' Cuirassiers] on the left wing made a disorderly retreat, much like a panicked flight. The Prince saw it from a hill and said aloud to his adjutants and the Brigade major De Rivecourt who were standing by him: 'Ha! Can you see those Dutchmen run?' To which De Rivecourt said: 'Excuse me, sir, but those are your cuirassiers, the States' army has no cuirassiers'. This is how the Prince was put in his place. He has never forgiven De Rivecourt for this remark.

Up with Orange and down with the French

The Pragmatic Army retreated into their winter quarters. With the Austrian Netherlands now under French control, that meant that for the first time, the vast majority of the Allied troops would be spending the winter months in the Republic. The commander of the States' forces, General Carl August Friedrich, Fürst zu Waldeck-Pyrmont (1704–1763) proposed to send 66 battalions and 92 squadrons to the frontier, of which 22 battalions would form the garrison of Maastricht, since this important city was strategically 'the key to Germany and the Republic'. The Council of State agreed for a large part with this proposition, but there were some points that had to be taken into consideration: the Council of State insisted that the majority of the troops stationed in Maastricht would be States' troops. Also, given the terrible reputation of the Austrian troops – more particularly the hussars, Croats and Pandours, that plundered and terrorised the local populace – they wanted as many of these removed from the Republic's territory as possible. Lastly, since peace negotiations were taking place in Breda, it was considered not the best idea to have British troops stationed there. In the end, the majority of the Austrian troops (62 battalions and 104 squadrons) were stationed in Luxemburg and around Liège; Maastricht would have a garrison of six Austrian and nine Dutch battalions, and the British battalions and squadrons would be sent to Brabant. The Hanoverian infantry was stationed along the

Meuse, while their cavalry was sent to Gelderland and Overijssel, as were the six Hessian battalions.

For the next campaign, the field army would number 40,000 Dutch, 40,000 British, and 60,000 Austrian troops; this 140,000-men-strong field army would be led by the Duke of Cumberland. Batthyányi would resume command of the Austrians, but Waldeck's position was uncertain: growing public unrest about the Allied defeats was used by the Orangist factions to try to have Waldeck removed, and have Prince Willem IV take his place. Cumberland openly declared his favour of Willem IV over Waldeck, although a member of the British court admitted there was no other capable commander available, since, as he wrote the Secretary to States General, 'all the others are imbecils'. Despite the fierce opposition of the Orangists, Waldeck, who they called 'a fool and a madman', was again elected to commander in chief of the Republic's forces. Some Orangist deputies protested, and a smear campaign ensued, but it was to no avail. General Isaac Baron Cronström (1665–1751) was replaced as commander of the infantry by the Bavarian general Ludwig Friederich von Saxen-Hildenburghausen (1710–1759). Lieutenant General Birkenfeld was also relieved from his command.

Meanwhile, the military situation had worsened, with French troops having advanced towards Bergen op Zoom in March. In a letter, read to the States General on 17 April, Louis XV had declared he could 'no longer spare the Republic's territory', and French troops would 'temporarily occupy the fortresses of the Republic until common sense had returned'; it was not a declaration of war, but an invasion was imminent. That same night, French troops under Lieutenant General Lowendahl entered Staats-Vlaanderen. De Saxe had no intent to invade Zeeland or Holland, and would rather advance towards Maastricht, but he knew the Allies would try to recapture Antwerp, and if he could capture the Scheldt, the attack would be a firm warning against the Republic. Accordingly, De Saxe attacked the fortresses and garrisons along the Scheldt. For the defence of two towns and five fortresses, a force of 15,000 men was needed, but the States' troops totalled no more than 3,800. Therefore, the French advance, although small, was a major success: the town of Sluis was captured on 22 April, Fort Ijzendijke on the 23rd, Fort De Parel on the 24 and Fort Liefkenshoek on the 25th, the latter seeing the Dutch garrison in a state of anarchy, 'being drunk and rebellious, having plundered all the houses', as described in a letter to Waldeck. Sas van Gent capitulated on the 30th, and Fort Philipine on 6 May. Panic among the local populace ensued; and the more the French advanced, the more the people in the streets openly called for the reinstatement of the Stadtholder. Riots and mob violence against the Republicans broke out, gangs of boys with orange cockades were out on the streets, shouting '*Oranje boven, de Fransen onder, die anders meent, die slaat de donder!*' ['Up with Orange, and down with the French, and those that say otherwise can go to hell!']. Known pro-French public figures were targeted at first, their houses plundered and themselves molested; but soon, anyone daring to go outside without an orange cockade or ribbon risked a severe beating by gangs of Orangist thugs who roamed the streets. Even the States General was stormed by an angry crowd, after rumours of a French naval landing in Holland.

The mob got what they wanted, and sooner than expected: already on 28 April, Zeeland elected Willem IV as Stadtholder; Holland and Utrecht elected him on 3 May, and Overijssel on May 10, making Willem IV the first ever to be elected Stadtholder of all provinces. What is more is that the title was now made hereditary, making the title monarchical. Five days later, having arrived in The Hague, he assumed the titles of Captain-General and Admiral of the Union, making him commander-in-chief of the army and navy. Maria van Antwerpen, the woman who served as grenadier Jan van Ant in Veldtmans' Regiment and was located in Zeeland, celebrated the event:

> [...] shortly after our arrival, the joyful announcement of the appointment of *His Highness the Prince of Orange,* as Stadtholder of this, and several other *Provinces,* was spread amongst the troops; among them, joy and happiness became widespread because of this appointment, it seemed that everyone's bravery and courage, even of the lowliest Soldier, grew because of it [...]; in short, there was none among us who wasn't willing and, with the greatest pleasure, able to give Life and Limb for that beloved Sovereign.

Schlippenbach, a fervent Orangist and personal friend of Willem IV, had high expectations:

> May the almighty God together with him grasp the reins of government and support his plans to save the fatherland, and rid the land of its oppressive fear. May God give him offspring who inherit his principles and emotions, to give the Republic a lasting peace, with thriving trade, a pure religion and everything that can aid in the happiness of the people. Blessings that the Republic would have never enjoyed if the government had been left in the hands of the divided States. [...] It is just to acknowledge with great joy what great fortune had come over the Republic by the appointment of H.S.H. the Prince of Orange as Stadtholder, and in conclusion, I join the cheer: *tandem bona causa triomphat!* [The Good Cause is victorious in the end].

The peace conference in Breda was discontinued. The British welcomed the appointment of Prince Willem IV as Stadtholder, since a separate peace between France and the Republic was now out of the question. But the relationship between the new Stadtholder and Britain was not ideal: he was not pleased with Cumberland's openly-expressed disdain for the States' troops, let alone that he resented Cumberland surpassing him as commander of the Allied forces. In return, it was clear that the 'prince of the mob', as they called him mockingly in London, surely had the ambitions to be as great as the King-Stadtholder Willem III, but proved to be nothing like his renowned predecessor. Although intelligent, he was indecisive, and any idea about the continuation of the war came from Orangist politicians. These had, strengthened by the reinstatement of the Stadtholder, called for a purge in all levels of government, to get rid of the Republicans once and for all. Willem, and especially his wife Anna of Hannover, daughter of George II, would have nothing of it: they were content with having seized power without any bloodshed, and support from the mob could not be the basis of his reign. Besides, the Republicans were now dependant on the favours of the Stadtholder anyway. Thus, even the most fervent opponent kept his position.

In the background, the French advance continued. They attacked Hulst and the surrounding fortresses, which was defended by a garrison of six Dutch and three British battalions and 250 dragoons, a total of 4,750 men, commanded by Lieutenant General De La Roque. Although the garrison was up to strength, and the first attacks were repelled with great vigour, the men in the outer defences of Fort Zandberg started mutinying, and when the drums struck roll call, they threw down their arms and declared they were no more willing to fight. The artillery commander panicked and had all the guns spiked. The troops in reserve now panicked and fled, leaving all their baggage and tents. De la Roque arrived too late in order to rally his men. He tried to launch a counter attack, but when the British commander refused, all was lost. He sent the British and three Dutch battalions to Axel, and remained with 2,000 troops in Hulst. However, before the French had started the siege properly, he surrendered the town on 11 May. He was allowed to withdraw with 400 men to Zeeland, while the rest were taken prisoner. On 17 May, Major General Soute surrendered Axel without firing a shot, and was given passage with his 2,200 men to Zeeland, leaving the whole of Staats-Vlaanderen now in French hands. These losses were a severe and humiliating blow for the new government, as well as for the army. De la Roque was called before a council of war and sentenced to death, which the indecisive Willem IV changed into lifelong imprisonment in Fort Loevestein. And all the time, Cumberland had done nothing, having 100,000 men in the field near Antwerp on 14 May but refusing to send reinforcements towards Zeeland. Any chance of recapturing Antwerp was now gone.

'Remember that you are the Guards' – The Battle of Lauffeld

It was impossible for the Republic to send enough troops to man the garrisons and organise a field army of 40,000 men, but Cumberland refused to spare any troops to strengthen the garrisons (save the three battalions at Hulst). His orders from London were clear: not to undertake any action unless victory was certain. On his and Batthyányi's initiative, the army took up positions along the Grote Nete river, thus threatening Brussels and Antwerp whilst securing the lines towards Maastricht. Waldeck sent Saxen-Hildenburghausen to Wuustwezel with a Dutch corps of 10 battalions and 28 squadrons, in order to secure the lines towards Holland and covering Bergen op Zoom. For three weeks, the armies waited for the French to advance, until, in June, the supplies were spent. Fortunately, King Louis XV had arrived at Brussels on 31 May, and he was eager to order his army forward. De Saxe had sat patiently behind his strong lines along the Dyle, but being reminded of his promise to Louis XV that he would take Maastricht and Bergen op Zoom this year, he reluctantly advanced towards Maastricht with his main force.

The Allies broke up camp on 24 June and moved towards Maastricht. The advance guard of the Allied army comprised of 18 battalions of infantry and 20 squadrons of cavalry, commanded by Count Leopold Joseph Daun (1705–1766); this force kept the French corps of the Prince of Clermont in check, trying to cut it off from the main French force and preventing it

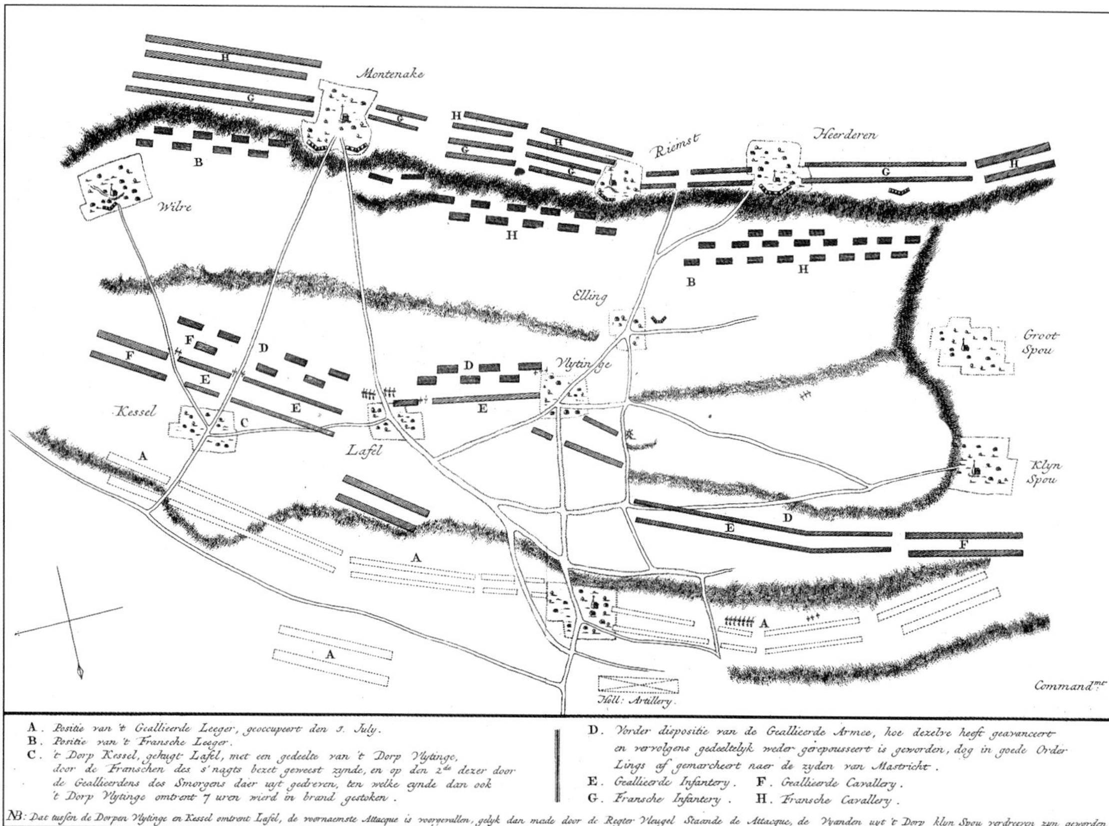

A map of the Battle of Lauffeld, with the positions of the armies on 1 and 2 July 1747. (Rijksmuseum)

from harassing the Allied advance. A skirmish on 29 June on the main road from Tongeren to Maastricht between light troops of both sides resulted in a stalemate. Waldeck, Cumberland, and Batthyányi decided to gather the army near Lanaken. The next day, the advance guard took the designated positions unopposed; Waldeck surveyed the terrain and found Clermont's corps still near Tongeren. The commanders decided to try and capture the heights near Tongeren, but during the night of 1 July, it was clear that De Saxe had joined Clermont. Waldeck heard of this, and noticed light troops were advancing on the flanks. The whole Allied army gathered and took up positions to prepare for battle; the 28 squadrons of cavalry, commanded by Lieutenant General Coenders, Major Generals Schack, Mattha, and Cannenburg, and Brigadiers Schlippenbach and Schagen, arrived at the gallop and joined the army on 1 July. On the morning of 2 July, Waldeck saw that both armies stood opposite each other. The army was drawn up in two lines between Kessel, Lauffeld, Vlytingen, and Klein Spouw, with the cavalry forming a third line behind the centre. Cumberland had somehow ignored the advice from General Ligonier to occupy these villages in his front: instead, they were burnt to the ground when the French retreated, leaving the British and Hanoverian troops in the open. It would prove to be a fatal mistake.

The French positions were obscured by the rolling countryside but, during the early hours, the French were amassing their troops on their right wing. At 8:00 a.m., two massive columns emerged, advancing towards Kessel and Lauffeld, and a third marching towards Vlytingen soon after that. The Allied reserve and advance guard, posted on the flanks, were recalled to the left wing; and Batthyányi sent a corps of Austrian cavalry in support, as did Waldeck, sending Mattha and Cannenburg with 15 squadrons. Lieutenant Colonel Baron van Duyn, a captain in the Dutch Horse Guards, told the troopers of his company 'to behave like men'. He had received a sabre cut across his arm and a carbine shot through the thigh during a skirmish several days earlier, but had refused to be taken to Maastricht, saying 'there was no need for it'. He urged his men: 'Remember that you are the Guards'.

When the French column reached Lauffeld at 10:00 a.m., a bitter fight ensued, in which in the four hours of hard fighting, the village changed sides five times until the British and Hanoverian troops finally had to give way to the overwhelming French forces. The Dutch cavalry counterattacked the French columns three times; General Trips charged with Frangipani's Hussars and scattered a French cavalry column supporting the infantry attack. Despite the fierce fighting, the villages were lost, and the Allied left wing had to retreat. Schlippenbach, with the 13 squadrons behind the centre, saw the Hessians in his front give way, while the French cavalry were advancing:

> Our squadrons did not want to await orders and retreated on their own initiative with haste. I shouted in vain to stop them. Suddenly, I was surrounded by a melee of Dutch and French horsemen, hacking into one another. A French cavalryman, wounded at the head by a sabre cut and covered in blood, came galloping at me like mad. I had my pistol in hand and the reins between my teeth. When he was close, I pulled the trigger and thought I had killed him. But he came even closer and shattered my nose with the hilt of his sabre. The French cannon kept firing, and one of the rounds shattered my horse's leg. I was thrown down, and could free myself only with the greatest effort. I sprained my hand doing so, but crawled back up and walked (without being followed) to the village of Kisselt, where I found two Dutch troopers bringing their equipment in order. I ordered them to let me ride one of their horses, which I managed with a lot of effort, since I couldn't move my hand. This is how I was brought to Maastricht, where I had my wounds treated.

The whole army slowly gave way, with a rear guard formed by six squadrons from the regiments Schack, Ginkel, Rechteren-Overijssel, and the Carabineers. Waldeck and Batthyányi met on the field; seeing how the French were not in pursuit, and hearing the Allied left wing soon would reach Maastricht, they decided to retreat the whole army there. Ten Dutch battalions and the Dutch artillery formed a column and began their retreat at 4:00 p.m., led by Cornabé's Free Companies and a combined grenadier battalion. They linked up with more Dutch cavalry, which formed a rear guard. Despite being under fire from the French artillery, the army retreated in good order and reached Maastricht.

The British, Hanoverians, and Hessians had borne the brunt of the fighting. James Woods, serving in the Royal Artillery, wrote in his diary:

> Being overpowered we were at last obliged to retreat something faster than we advanced and in our retreating we left nine 3-pounders, six short 6-pounders, one long 6-pounder with three colours and a kettledrum.

Although the Austrian battalions had not moved and retreated without firing a shot, the Dutch shared in the blame:

> We lost more of the artillery people that day than ever was known at any battle before, but if the Dutch had done their duty and the Austrians had come in to back us we should certainly have won the day, but was obliged to retreat as far as Maastricht and lay on our arms that night. If it had not been for the town that covered our retreat, we should certainly have been all taken prisoner.

The States' contingent lost 537 men and 844 horses, along with three standards of the regiments Schack, Rechteren, and Schlippenbach. Among the dead was Lieutenant Colonel Baron van Duyn, having been hit by a cannonball during the retreat. The total losses for the Pragmatic Army were about 5,000 men and several guns. But for the French, their Pyrrhic victory had cost them over 10,000 men; especially the Irish regiments were hit hard, suffering 1,900 casualties including over 80 officers. The Allies had taken up strong positions around Maastricht, and in the next two weeks, the Free Companies of Cornabé and Frangipani's Hussars would wage a bloody guerrilla war against the French. A siege was now out of the question. De Saxe positioned his army opposite the Allied forces and sent Lowendahl with 20,000 men to Bergen op Zoom, hoping this diversion would prompt the Allies to divide their forces.

The Siege of Bergen op Zoom

Bergen op Zoom was the key to Holland and Zeeland. It had been besieged and stormed in 1588, 1605 and 1622, but never taken, hence its nickname 'La Pucelle' – 'the virgin'. Its fortifications had been modernised by the famous Dutch engineer Menno van Coehoorn, and it had the reputation of being impregnable. A 5.5 kilometre line, built in 1727, connected the town to Forts Moermont, Prinssen, and De Roovere, all the way to the fortified town of Steenbergen.

News of the French advance reached The Hague on 9 July. The States General and the Council of State sent out a declaration to the local populace, demanding they take whatever provisions they had and store them in Willemstad and Breda, so as to not let anything fall into enemy hands. It was decided to increase the number of troops for the defence of Bergen op Zoom to 17,000 men: 4,500 in Bergen op Zoom, 1,600 in Steenbergen, and 17,000 in reserve along the Bergen op Zoom – Steenbergen line. Cronström was appointed as commander of this force the next day, despite his protests that he was too old and too infirm. That same day, Lowendahl's troops entered the fortress of Zandvliet, the 900 man garrison of which had left that evening after a token resistance, having suffered two dead and two injured. The French then advanced unopposed and arrived before Bergen op Zoom on 12 July. They occupied the area from the sea in the east towards the

Map of the siege of Bergen op Zoom. In the north the besieged Fort De Roovere. Behind it the Allied reserve camp. (Rijksmuseum)

village of Wouw, and opened the first parallel during the night of 14–15 July. Cronström had arrived in Bergen op Zoom that same day and immediately inspected the troops and defences. There were not enough men in Steenbergen (900) and Bergen op Zoom (3,600), and there were not enough artillerymen, sappers and miners available. Even worse: Cronström's arrival led to friction in command. The governor, General Willem Ludwig Prince of Hessen-Phillipsthal (1680–1760), felt he was pushed aside; and the cavalry commanders, Austrian Lieutenant General Philibert and the Hanoverian Major General Montigny, were reluctant to take orders, saying they were under direct command of Saxen-Hildenburghausen. They even demanded their squadrons would be shipped to Tholen. But Saxen-Hildenburghausen declared he had no objection to serving under Cronström, so that put an end to the matter. It was urgent to come up with a plan for a counterattack. The cavalry commanders however were unwilling to risk a battle in the open field. Hessen-Phillipsthal was therefore ordered to harass the enemy with several small sorties in the meantime.

Already on the 20th, the French opened the second parallel, and started a relentless bombardment of the town, targeting houses and public buildings. By doing this, Lowendahl hoped the garrison would soon lose heart and surrender. He had little time, since there were hardly any provisions to be found, nor could any be brought up over the Scheldt. Those inhabitants that had not fled the town, suffered the most, their houses being destroyed by the many incendiary rounds fired by the French; Jacques Lejeune, one of the inhabitants of Bergen op Zoom, wrote in a letter to his wife:

> No heathens, nor Turks, nor any barbaric nation there is, could have behaved worse, for whenever [the French] have caused a fire somewhere, or notice one, they throw hundreds of bombs towards it, to prevent it being put out.

But this made the inhabitants even more resolved that the town would not be taken, as an anonymous author, known as 'An English Volunteer', wrote:

> The Town being already almost ruined, the Inhabitants had nothing further to fear for their Effects: All the Danger they could now apprehend respecting only their Persons, they were unanimously resolved to perish in the Place, rather than yield, Revenge glowing in the Breast of every true *Dutchman,* and, if possible, a greater Desire to ruin the *French* Army than even save the Town.

Slowly but surely, the French lines came ever closer, a third parallel being opened on the 22nd, and a fourth on the 28th, despite the Allied troops putting up a steady fire and showering the attackers with up to 5,000 hand grenades every day. A French attack on Steenbergen on the 24 had failed, whilst Fort De Roovere was now also besieged. Cronström and Hessen-Phillipsthal realised they needed help from outside to withstand the French. They wrote to Cumberland on 31 July, urging him to send reinforcements, but he and Batthyányi argued they had already done their part by sending Waldeck with 8,000 men. Waldeck arrived at Bois-le-Duc on the 30th, only to learn that Cronström had been appointed commander, so there was little else for him to do than return to Maastricht and take command of the Dutch troops there. Since the Orangist factions had come to power, his position had already become untenable. He handed over command to Lieutenant General Baron Thoe Schwarzenberg en Hohenlandsberg (1693–1757), and, without sending a letter of resignation, he left the army and returned to his castle at Arolson. The Republic thus lost one of its most energetic commanders.

Schwarzenberg continued towards Oudenbosch; five battalions and four squadrons joined his command, and when news arrived in Bergen op Zoom that he was underway, Philibert and Montigny joined him with 16 squadrons. With the addition of two battalions from Breda, the relief force numbered 17 battalions and 36 squadrons: about 13,000 troops. This would suffice to drive away the French, whose losses were mounting due to the continuous fighting, disease, and desertion. A plan for an attack by the relief force, with a simultaneous counterattack with 14 battalions from Bergen op Zoom, was drawn up. Philibert and Montigny however refused to cooperate, saying the terrain was not suitable for cavalry, and having doubts about the success of the

The bombardment of Bergen op Zoom on August 1st 1747. Print by Simon Fokke, after 1747. (Rijksmuseum)

attacks. It was decided to keep the force at Oudenbosch, and have the cavalry harass the French supply lines from Antwerp. Prince Willem IV was very displeased when he heard of it. His reputation as the saviour of the Republic would again suffer a severe blow. Since the Allied forces matched those of the French in numbers of battalions and squadrons, he urged the commanders to take action, and ignore the over-cautious cavalry commanders.

On the French side, Lowendahl was also growing impatient: three weeks of massive bombardments from 73 cannon, 70 mortars and 22 howitzers had not led to the surrender of the town. In order to put more pressure on the defenders, he ordered the defences to be stormed. On August 5, at 11:00 p.m., the French engineers detonated three mines, which was followed by ten companies of grenadiers storming the walls. Lejeune wrote how at first, the attackers managed to break through, 'under the terrifying screams of *Vive le Roi*! and *Tue en tue*!, to which ours answered: *Vivat Orange en de Staten*! [Long live Orange and the States]'. Soon however, the French grenadiers came under heavy fire from all sides. When two mines exploded under the French positions, 'throwing up the bodies straight into the air, and we could not see where they landed', the attackers withdrew, having gained little, but lost over 33 dead and 428 wounded. Lowendahl would not risk another attack soon. Cronström came up the next day with a plan for a series of attacks on the French troops, driving them from Wouw and Fort De Roovere, whilst simultaneously attacking from Bergen op Zoom to break through the siege lines. In order for this plan to have success, the attackers would have to make haste and not bother with taking prisoners, but rather attack any enemy in sight, in order to make sure Lowendahl could not unite his troops. Others however were more cautious and suggested the Austrian light cavalry would harass the French supply lines. Already, the French had trouble supplying bread and drinking water, and cutting off the lines from Antwerp would force them to give up. After long debates, it was decided that Wouw would be attacked in the early hours of 10 August by an advance guard; if the French were driven out, the main army would follow.

The plan was to attack Wouw from three sides. Three battalions arrived at night from the direction of Roosendaal in the north-east, took up their positions, and attacked the village as planned. However, the main force of grenadiers and free companies, coming from Nispen in the south-east, arrived at dawn, after the attacks of the first columns had already failed, and their attacks were also repulsed by the French troops with ease. The third column, coming from Steenbergen in the north-west, arrived even later: they marched towards the sound of the guns, but when the firing stopped, their commander halted them and withdrew. Because of bickering over command, the cavalry never took part in the operation. The Allies lost 86 dead, 139 wounded, and 21 missing. Cronström waited for the message from Schwarzenberg to bring his troops forward from the line, but at 2:00 p.m., he realised the attacks had failed. His only hope now was that Cumberland and Batthyányi would at long last come to the relief of Bergen op Zoom. But the only reinforcements that were sent were four engineers and a captain with 72 artillerymen from the British contingent, followed by three Austrian NCOs with 71 artillerymen and miners, and later a British officer with 34 miners. These were excellent troops, who could have been used much earlier, but it was too little, too late.

The relentless bombardments began to take their toll on the defences of Bergen op Zoom, which were severely damaged. Countermines were detonated, destroying the French mines and siege lines. Sorties attacked trenches and artillery platforms, whilst the artillery bombarded the attackers. The French were kept at bay at the cost of 30,000 pounds of gunpowder every day, and worse: the daily loss of 50 to 60 casualties. The dire situation was worsened for Cronström by the animosity among his subordinates, and the meddling of Prince Willem IV. The Stadtholder urged him to attack, and sent detailed plans on how to trap the French in a pincer movement. Cronström however was not pleased with the Stadtholder's daring plans, concocted in the comforts of his residence in The Hague, whilst Cronström was cramped in a bedroom with his staff. His answer was simple: only the arrival of the field army could drive the French away. Prince Willem IV wrote to Cumberland on the 16th requesting him to immediately march towards Bergen op Zoom. He instructed the commander of the garrison of Maastricht, Lieutenant General Hobbe Baron Aylva (1696–1772) to send 10 Dutch battalions if Cumberland refused. The letter arrived on the 19th, the same day Batthyányi received orders from Maria Theresia to keep his forces around Maastricht, whatever the cost. The next day, Cumberland, now also under pressure from London to take action, held a conference with his generals, to which Aylva and his staff were not invited. They concluded that the march towards the relief of Bergen op Zoom was impossible, and only a force of 15 battalions plus six squadrons of dragoons and 100 hussars were sent, commanded by the Austrian General Charles-Urbain Count Chanclos de Rets Brisuila (1686–1761).

Mines were sprung on 19, 20, and 21 August, destroying large parts of the defences. The defenders feared the French might try to storm the town on 25

August, the day of Saint Louis, so preparations were made. As expected, 'all hell broke loose', as described by Pieter Johan van As (1722–1801), an ensign in Kinschot's Regiment. The bombardments that started at midnight evoked scenes, similar to the horrors of World War One:

> The stench we had to endure at [the lunette] *Zeeland* was unspeakable. Because of the many bombs fired at us, many corpses that had been buried there for several weeks, were now thrown up from the ground in pieces.

A countermine was detonated:

> The heat we felt when the mine exploded – being only 21 paces away, – was impossible to comprehend. All the ovens which I had faced, as they say, be it for melting lead, iron or glass, are incomparable with such a mine.

The French, thinking it was their mine that had exploded, stormed the defences, but were beaten back time and again.

> One hour after the storming of the lunette *Zeeland* had been ceased, I stood in front of the gabions, to have a look at how the situation was, when an enemy cannonball hit the top of the gabions and, ricocheting, flew over my head. The wind blew my hat off. This caused such a dizziness, that, no matter how I held on to the gabions, I fell to the floor, and next to an old Scots soldier, who had experienced this before, and grabbed me by the head and started rubbing for about half an hour, until my dizziness was gone.

At the end of the day, Van As had lost 16 men of the 30 men he commanded. Despite the heavy fighting and the destruction of the defences, morale was high. 'On our Part,' the anonymous English volunteer wrote,

> [N]othing is omitted that may contribute to keep the Spirits of the Soldiers. Besides their Provisions, of which they have all the Plenty they can wish, and every thing perfectly good in its Kind, every Man who ventures to fetch off a Gabion from the *French,* receives for Recompence a Crown immediately. This encourages them wonderfully, and inspires some of them with so much Intrepidity that they make light of fetching one after another, notwithstanding the Fire of the Besiegers.

Despite his age and health, Cronström toured the town on horseback every day, to inspire his men. Provisions and money, donated from all over the Republic, were delivered daily, whilst the French soldiers went days without bread. Lowendahl had requested that the French be given time to bury their dead, but, since he mercilessly bombarded the city, this was denied. Thus the bodies of the attackers lay 'rotting by Thousands like dead Dogs before the Fortifications'. In order to intimidate the French even further, the defenders did not shoot the wounded, who they could clearly see among the dead. Instead of putting them out of their misery, they let them cry out in agony and perish on the spot. French deserters were rounded up by the hundreds. A letter from a French general, intercepted by Austrian hussars, told of the dire situation, and concluded that Bergen op Zoom could never be taken. The letter was read aloud to the men to bolster their spirit. To even further intimidate the French, Cronström ordered a massive counter bombardment on 1 September, the birthday of the Stadtholder, 'which lasted from Morning till Night [...]. Our Batteries &c. were hung with Orange-coloured Ribbons, and the Mouths of our Bombs painted of the same Colour, that the Enemy might know on what Occasion they were sent'.

Chanclos had meanwhile reached Oudenbosch on 31 August and took command of the combined forces. He was unwilling to request the main army being sent to the relief of Bergen op Zoom, and signed a report in which it was said that the French would need at least until the end of September to take the town. Cumberland and Batthyányi, satisfied by this report, ordered Chanclos to strengthen the garrison with his fresh battalions, in order to harass the French siege lines. Hessen-Phillipsthal believed the French could be kept at bay by these attacks, but Cronström feared the French would need far less time to capture the town. He ordered that the garrison would prepare for a retreat. He could only hope that Lowendahl would lose his nerve and have his troops attack the town, which would certainly cost him dearly.

Lowendahl was indeed desperate: with the siege two months underway, the campaign season drew to an end. It would not be long before the weather would turn foul, with rain flooding the trenches, worsening the already hopeless situation. Continuation of the siege 'by the book' would certainly mean his army, now 80,000 strong, would be ruined. He decided on one last gamble: to storm the town and drive the defenders out. On 16 September, at 4:00 a.m., a massive bombardment heralded several massive attacks. Caught by surprise, the defenders fought off the attacks with the bayonet, until they were forced to retreat. When Hessen-Phillipsthal sounded the alarm, it was already too late: the French troops were inside the town and were now engaged in hand-to-hand combat in the streets. The Saxe-Gotha Regiment defended the headquarters in the Markiezenhof and drove the attackers back, supported later by the 2nd Waldeck Battalion and Mattha's Dragoons. On the Market Square, the regiments of Colyear and Deutz counterattacked the French twice, but were driven back. As more and more French troops poured in, Cronström ordered the retreat. Apart from 200 men of Van Rechteren's Regiment, the whole garrison and the reserve force behind the line abandoned the town and escaped to safety, leaving behind several hundred dead. The French captured 1,200 men, most of them wounded. Lowendahl had managed to turn a certain defeat into a triumph, with the loss of only 137 dead and 260 wounded. The overall losses however made the siege of Bergen op Zoom the bloodiest of the war. The Allies had lost about 5,500 men, while the French casualties may have numbered close to 20,000 men.

While the Allied troops retreated towards Steenbergen, Oudenbosch and Tholen, the French troops were given two days to ransack the town. Lowendahl's men were out of control. The tales of those who witnessed it gave descriptions of savagery which had not been seen again since the Thirty Years War: men, women, children and even babies were butchered. What was left of the town was burned to the ground. The reports shocked everyone, including Louis XV, who asked De Saxe for advice. De Saxe answered that

The plundering of Bergen op Zoom, print dated 1747. (Anne S.K. Brown Collection)

the King must either have Lowendahl hanged for the atrocities committed, or promote him to Marshal of France for his remarkable feat. Louis chose the latter, and left the army on 23 September; the campaign was over, as far as he was concerned.

In the weeks that followed, the French secured their victory by taking the last remaining fortresses along the Scheldt, and then went into their winter quarters. When Fort Lillo surrendered, Ensign Van As, who had been transferred from Bergen op Zoom early in September, was captured. While he was escorted into captivity in France, the French troops retreated into their winter quarters.

Cronström wrote a journal about his experiences during the siege. He concluded:

> I was determined to make no proposition, nor have one made, to surrender either the town or a fort of the line, but to hold out the defence as long as possible; although it was clear that we would have to submit in the end, because we had no hope of receiving any help from outside, since those who were not involved in the siege comforted themselves with the thought that the town would hold out without trouble, and could wear out the besiegers, so that they would abandon the siege, according to the rumour that was spread in Holland, but which was never the intention of Count Lowendahl. I had notified His Highness and the Duke of Cumberland repeatedly that the town would surrender in the end. I had not shown the sadness I felt about that, other than to Mr Verelst, the State Representative in the Field, to whom I said several days before our misfortune (and who surely will recall that), that while everyone expected us to be able to withstand the siege of the town, and I saw not the least possibility to preserve her, I hoped for my sake to die in the affair.

Had Cronström surrendered the town on, or just before, the 16th, he would have been heralded as a great commander, having successfully defended the town for 58 days. Instead, Cronström was accused of having failed his duty – among others by Cumberland and Willem IV, eager to divert attention from their own neglect. Both demanded an inquiry of the affair. To add insult to injury, the army at Oudenbosch was afterwards strengthened with 17 battalions, 10 squadrons and 214 artillerymen, with Batthyányi taking over command.

2

Downfall

Rebuilding the Army

The fall of Bergen op Zoom came as a shock through all of Europe. For the Republic, it was painfully clear she could expect little from her allies. Maastricht and Breda were the only bulwarks left. Maastricht was an outpost and was regarded as lost; if Breda fell, only Holland would be safe behind a strong defensive line, whilst the French armies could march unhindered through Staats-Brabant, Gelderland, and Utrecht. The army of the Republic had only 26 battalions and 64 squadrons left that were intact.

Willem IV remained optimistic, and tried to convince everyone that the Republic was still determined to continue the war. A two percent property tax that had been levied in September under the name of *Liberale Gift* [Generous Donation] would raise several million guilders for the war effort. The fifth augmentation, which had passed on 29 May 1747, was already well underway, with German and Swiss troops arriving, and other regiments being organised. The augmentation consisted of the following:

Infantry regiments:	**Battalions**	**Total**
Wurzburg	2	1,600
Drumlanrig	2	1,760
Hessen	3	2,400
Nassau	4	3,520
Cornabé	1	880
Saksen-Hildenburghausen	1	880
Hessen-Darmstadt	2	1,620
Imhoff	1	880
Leutrum	1	880
Lillers	1	880
Baden-Durlach	1	880
Totleben	1	880
Schwarzburg	2	1,200
Baden-Baden	2	1,200
Braunschweig-Wolfenbüttel	3	2,400

Swiss Regiments	**Battalions**	**Total**
Graffenriedt	3	2,400
Charles Stürler	3	2,400
Chambrier	3	2,400
Bude	3	2,400
Guards	2	1,600
Zwitsersche Jagers (three coys)		150

Dragoons	**Squadrons**	**Total**
Hessen	4	640
D'Olne	5	750

Free Companies	**Total**
Gilliard	122
Pouilly de Ginvri	300
De Vial	502
Buhlman	200
Cornabé Dragoons	100
Cornabé Hussars	100

Artillery	**Companies**	**Total**
	4	996

With an addition of five infantry companies and two guard companies, that made a total of 37,594 men.

The cavalry regiments had not suffered many losses, and could easily be replenished; the infantry regiments however had been severely mauled, most having lost half their numbers or more; 15,000 troops had been taken prisoner. A general pardon was given to all deserters, giving them the opportunity to return to their regiments. Given that new recruits were hard to find within the Republic itself, a plan was made to reorganise the undermanned regiments into battle-ready units: what was left of 27 regiments, now designated as *debris*, was amalgamated into 14 battalions, which could be ready for action within two months. 11 *debris* regiments, and the remainder which were still intact, were ordered to fill the ranks with new recruits, so as to have a field battalion of at least 800 men ready. The strength of the army on paper was now 106 battalions and 75 squadrons, or 110,000 men, to which 15,000 Russians would be added. According to Willem IV, the Republic could easily organise a field army of 70,000 men, including the Russian contingent, and expected that Britain and Austria would do the same.

Britain however had little hope of winning the war: although it had always supported the reinstatement of the Stadtholder, the eagerness of Willem IV and the Orangists to continue the war was now standing in the way of peace and London felt quite uncomfortable with this aggressive tone. Cumberland, always the critic, stated the Stadtholder 'overrated his strength' and openly expressed disdain for both him and his troops. Britain therefore would only continue the war if the Republic could guarantee that the 70,000 troops were indeed available, if an inquiry into the fall of Bergen op Zoom was made, and if the Republic would officially declare war on France. The latter was refused outright by Willem IV, who in turn demanded that British troops would also man the garrisons. The hard work by diplomats finally paid off: although hesitant, the British were in the end convinced to send troops, albeit no more than 63,000 men.

The Stadtholder had deliberated with Cumberland and Batthyányi about the plans for the next campaign. With the towns of Maastricht and Breda under direct threat, the Allied forces would be gathered there, with a screen of irregular troops along the front to prevent being surprised by the French. Cumberland reckoned that, after subtracting the forces needed to man the garrisons and fortresses, keeping a reserve in Zeeland, and keeping incomplete units in mind, the Allies could still bring 170,000 troops in the field, which were to be divided into three corps: a main force of 32,000 Austrians and 42,000 British, Hanoverians, and Hessians near Maastricht under Chanclos; a secondary force 32,000 Dutch, 20,000 Russians and 8,000 Austrians near Breda, commanded by the Austrian Field Marshal Ludwig Ernst Duke of Braunschweig-Lüneburg-Bevern (1718–1788); and a reserve corps of 10,000 Russians, 14,000 Austrians, and 6,000 irregular troops in Luxemburg. If possible, the main force would march unto Brussels and lay siege to it, whilst the secondary force could cut off Bergen op Zoom. The Allies needed two large siege trains and plenty of supplies for this task. A military convention was finally agreed upon on 26 January 1748. According to the latest reports, the Allies would have almost 200,000 men at the ready in Flanders to drive the French out – or at least convince them to sue for peace. Although this was an optimistic scenario, many knew that it was also the last chance to turn the tide in favour of the Allies: it had to be done now, or all was lost.

When Cumberland arrived in March in The Hague to prepare for the next campaign, he sensed something was wrong. All of a sudden, the Republic needed a loan of one million pounds to finance the army, and Willem IV had declared that peace was the only option if the Republic was to survive. He was furious about the sudden change of heart of the Stadtholder, who had slowly been convinced to opt for peace negotiations; for Cumberland, it was clear that his sister Anna was the reason Willem IV had become pacifist. In reality, Willem IV was deeply frustrated: he had hoped that a victory at Bergen op Zoom would be the beginning of his glorious career as saviour of the nation. That myth had been shattered by the refusal of Cumberland and Batthyányi to send a relief force. Furthermore, he had hoped to lead an army in the coming campaign, after having been refused a command for years by the Republicans. But even though he had reluctantly agreed to serve under Cumberland – something Anna was furious about – the British still refused to have British troops man the garrisons. Everything he had given up for the greater good, every insult (according to him) he had to take, had led to nothing, and thus he had grown weary of those convincing him to continue the war. The Republicans, seeing how the increased war efforts bled the country dry, seized the opportunity to regain their influence, after having to keep quiet in order to avoid the Orangist wrath. To save the Republic, and save the army, there had to be a peace agreement, preferably before the campaign started. Obstructing the formation of the army near Breda, and thus possibly losing Maastricht, was a risk they were willing to take.

To Cumberland's frustration, he was not given any information concerning the actual numbers of the Dutch army. Worse was the news that the regiments had not yet been assembled near Breda; the armies would not gather this month to start their offensive. By April, he learned that the Dutch contingent would not have 32,000 men available, but 10,000 at most by the end of that month. Therefore, he was compelled to send 19 allied battalions of his own command in order to defend Breda. The sudden and extensive increase of the army with the Fifth Augmentation made it difficult to find enough recruits: as time went on, premiums rose, whilst recruits enlisted for one year only, or two at most. It also attracted several roguish types, such as a certain Count Totleben, whose biography by the popular writer F.L. Kersteman appeared in 1761:

> He, and other Adventurers, who came flying in in droves from *France, Germany* and elsewhere, thought they would do great service to the *Republic,* and what feats of heroism these fortune seekers have done was proven in all clarity by the World famous exploits of the likes of a *Frangipani,* a *De Vial,* and this *Totleben* [...]. Mister Totleben, who cashed in on his shining title in Holland, arrived at court with great splendour; [...] he was said to be a man of noble birth, who was seeking a considerable commission.

After a lengthy talk with the Stadtholder, he was promised a colonelcy and a regiment of infantry:

> While the Count had promised [the Stadtholder] to raise and arm that regiment at his own expense, and because he had stipulated in the capitulation that he would appoint his own officers, the greedy Adventurer wielded his arbitrary power, so as to improperly enrich himself; he made this commission into a goldmine; his abuse of it however, was the cause of many disturbances: because not only did the cunning Colonel sell more captaincies and commissions than he could provide for, he favoured the highest bidders, who often proved the most incompetent.

While his officers sought recruits in Germany, Count Totleben spent his new fortune on a high society lifestyle among the upper class families of Gelderland. Eventually, his luck would run out: a scandal (he almost committed bigamy), rumours of his involvement in the murder of his major, the many complaints from his officers, and increasing threats from his creditors, made him flee to The Hague; but his notoriety having preceded him, he was no longer welcome at court.

It was clear that the armies near Breda and Maastricht would never be assembled. The final straw was the news of the arrival of Marshal De Saxe in Brussels, which meant a French advance was imminent. Those at the British court who believed that a campaign was still possible lost whatever little credibility they still had when Willem IV bluntly remarked that the Republic could not pay its share in the financing of the Russian contingent. It is true that there were enough funds on paper, but in reality a large sum of the *Liberale Gift* had not yet been levied, Staats-Brabant and the area around Bergen op Zoom were in French hands and could not be taxed, and the rapid expansion of the army and the fleet was a costly affair: there simply was no cash available to pay the troops nor the labourers working on the defences. In London, everyone was now convinced that peace was absolutely necessary; the Stadtholder had lost all goodwill. With the Austrian Netherlands occupied by the French, the Republic had little to negotiate with. The Dutch deputy to the States General Willem Count Bentinck van Rhoon (1704–1774), who travelled to Aix-la-Chapelle to attend the preliminary peace negotiations, feared the worst: it was very well possible he would receive instructions to make peace with France without Britain and Austria.

The Siege of Maastricht

As was feared, the French began their advance against Maastricht on 1 April. The army had gathered around Brussels a few days before. It was organised into seven columns, each about 10–11,000 strong, of which five would march towards Maastricht. All commanders had received strict, detailed orders, with all the marching routes given. After having created a diversion, the army advanced with great speed, reaching Tongeren on the 7th. Chanclos, who had left Maastricht on the 3rd, withdrew his corps further towards Roermond the next day. By the 11th, the French troops had encircled Maastricht; the first trenches were opened on the 15th. Their main objective would be the northern front of the town. De Saxe had set up his headquarters in the abbey of Hocht, north of the town; Lowendahl set up his at Borgharen castle, north of Wyck, on the other shore of the Meuse. Both were connected by two pontoon bridges.

The garrison, commanded by Lieutenant General Aylva, consisted of 4,800 Austrians and Bavarians, and 5,000 Dutch troops including 300 artillerymen and two companies of miners. A garrison of that size could withstand the besiegers; the Dutch contingent however included 3,400 men of nine *debris* regiments, and some of these were in a terrible state: of Oudshoorn's Regiment, a detachment of 38 privates, two sergeants and six cadets had arrived without weapons and hardly any clothing. After the regiments of Halkett and Maleprade, and Gillard's Free Company had left on 3 April to join the corps near Breda, the only complete regiment present was that of d'Envie.

Aylva and his staff decided to launch a counterattack on the second parallel in the evening of 17 April. Three columns would attack simultaneously at 11:00 p.m., under cover of heavy artillery fire: on the left, a combined force of three *debris* regiments Aylva, La Rivière, and Du Vergé, about 500 men strong; in the centre seven Austrian and Bavarian grenadier companies, about 400 men; and on the right a combined force of 500 Austrian musketeers. Behind

A volunteer *Jager* during the siege of Maastricht, 1748. Dark green uniform, dark green cap with brass plate, black belts. Presumably the *Jaeger Kompanie* attached to Chambrier's Regiment (see part I). (Vinkhuijzen Collection)

the troops were 700 labourers ready to follow the troops and demolish the trenches. Aylva and the other generals watched the whole operation from a bastion nearby. The preparations were in order, but the attack was postponed to midnight, because the Austrian engineer commander had disappeared, only to emerge later, completely drunk. By then, it had started snowing heavily, and the men were frozen to the bone by the time the order to advance was given. The Dutch column stumbled across the slippery ground, whereby some fell, taking others with them; several muskets were fired by accident, which caused a panic among the inexperienced soldiers. In the end they retreated to their starting point. The Austrian musketeers on the right fared not much better: they reached the second parallel, but fled after the first shots were fired at them. Aylva feared the grenadiers in the centre would not succeed without support; he ordered all the soldiers on watch duty to be gathered and kept in reserve. The centre column however was successful: the grenadiers reached the second parallel without much resistance and drove the French off. The labourers then followed and managed to destroy 600 yards of trenches. After 90 minutes, the labourers and grenadiers retreated back into the town. The Allies had lost six dead and 76 wounded, 18 of which were Dutch and Bavarian.

Map of the siege of Maastricht, 1748. (Rijksmuseum)

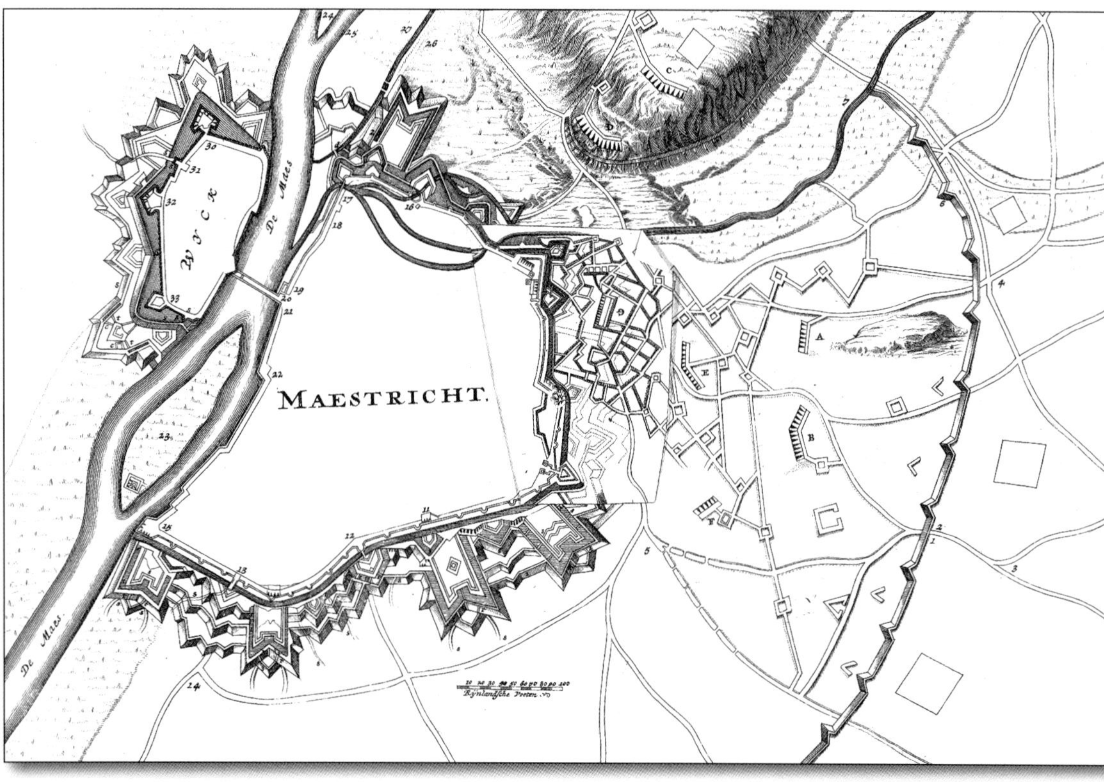

The French had lost three dead and 47 wounded. The troops had initially panicked and run away, and it took some time before they could be organised to drive the attackers off. For four days, the work in the trenches stopped. By now, the foul weather began to take its toll: the men had little cover against the snow, and in some places, they stood up to their knees in the mud. On 21 April, the artillery emplacements were ready, and the bombardment from over 100 cannon began. The weather, however, affected the mortars and howitzers, and many projectiles did not explode. That evening, two heavy laden ships, filled with hay, were set adrift by the garrison; these were moored too close to a gate, and it was feared they would catch fire during an attack. Coincidentally, the ships rammed through one of the pontoon bridges that connected the headquarters of De Saxe and Lowendahl. The second bridge was opened but it was also damaged, and the strong current of the Meuse made it impossible to close it again. The miners and sappers, who had their quarters on the eastern shore, had to be ferried over now. The next day, the French staff decided to cease any work on the trenches during the night. The snowfall was replaced by heavy rain. The difficulties were mounting for the French besiegers; a new pontoon bridge being finished on the 24th, was a small comfort.

Inside the town, the Allied generals planned another sortie, this time against the artillery batteries on the eastern shore, which were doing a lot of damage. Four companies of grenadiers, 600 infantry, and 50 to 60 volunteers to disable the guns, would attack from Wyck in three columns, supported by an attack of 150 Austrian cavalry between the two parallels. The troops were brought in position on the night of 27 April at 1:30 a.m., where they waited in silence until the sign for the attack would be given at daybreak. When the signal came, the troops marched forward unopposed in perfect order. The volunteers managed to disable 18 cannon and six mortars, destroy several gun carriages, and damage the emplacements. When the French reinforcements arrived, the troops retreated in good order, keeping the enemy at bay with volley fire. The Allies had lost 50 dead and wounded. The attack however had little effect, and by the end of the 28th, the French had managed to have most pieces firing again. The next day, at 10 PM, the French launched an attack against a bastion with 10 grenadier companies; they managed to capture a flêche, since the mines underneath it had not detonated. Lieutenant Colonel Bourquin, the highest ranking officer present of the newly organised regiment of Sappers and Miners, decided to inspect the mines himself the next evening. He and his detachment of miners however walked right into the second French attack, and a volley killed him and his men immediately. The French continued their attack and managed to capture another fleche. On the 30th, the miners detonated several mines under the French positions, with devastating effect: half the French grenadiers there were killed or wounded. In total, these attacks had cost the French 50 dead and 300 wounded; they requested a short ceasefire. From 5:00 to 6:00 p.m., both sides recovered their dead and wounded.

Whilst Maastricht was under siege, Cumberland gathered whatever troops he could find around Roermond. Still, even including Chanclos' Austrians, he had no more than 45,000 men at the ready; it was expected that De Saxe would have three times that number by the end of the month. Cumberland decided that he would retreat towards Eindhoven and Bois-le-Duc and unite his force with the Dutch troops that were underway. However, when by 28 April there had been no more than 28,000 troops gathered, the whole force was sent to take up defensive positions near Eindhoven, to cover Grave and Breda. There would be no relief force to come to the aid of Maastricht, apart from a force of light troops that was sent across the Meuse to harass the French supply lines. The Free Companies, Croats, Pandours and Hussars managed to reach Zutendaal and Gelik by May, where they set up camp and thus posed a serious threat. 400 French hussars were sent to intercept them, but it seems they had been warned as when the French reached Zutendaal, the corps was already gone. Batthyányi had asked Daun to look at the possibility of sending a relief force. Daun reported on the 30th that there was a combined force of Austrian, British and Hanoverian troops ready, 66 battalions and 107 squadrons in total; but that this would not suffice to drive the French besiegers away. He therefore suggested that an open battle should be avoided, and the defenders do their utmost to hold Maastricht until the Russian contingent would arrive.

Prince Willem IV arrived at Breda on 2 May to take over command of the Dutch troops that had gathered there. By then, a preliminary peace had already been signed on 30 April; Cumberland had not awaited his approval, but sent a courier to Maastricht, ordering Aylva to surrender the town. The French had also learned of these latest developments; they halted their approach on 3 May and requested a ceasefire. At first, the defenders denied that request until, in the late afternoon, the courier had reached Aylva. However, he refused to give up the town, since he wanted to have direct approval of Willem IV himself. De Saxe agreed with a ceasefire to await the answer of the Stadtholder. Aylva received two letters on the 6th: the first was a personal letter from the Prince, stating he was pleased with Aylva's conduct and that he was appointed governor of Maastricht for life; the second instructed him to either have Maastricht occupied by a joined Dutch and French garrison, or by neutral troops. But during negotiations, it was clear that De Saxe would only accept a complete surrender. On the 7th, Aylva ordered the white flag be raised. He visited De Saxe the next day at his headquarters at Hocht Abbey, and preparations were made to hand over the town. By then, the first French officers were already roaming the town to find decent quarters.

On 10 May, the garrison marched out with drums beating and colours flying, the Dutch bearing the orange cockade on their hats. The Dutch and Bavarians marched towards Bois-le-Duc, with Aylva at their head; behind him were four guns and two mortars, a courtesy of De Saxe. The Austrians marched towards Tongeren. The Dutch and Bavarians had lost 385 dead and wounded, the Austrians had suffered 454 casualties. At 11:00 a.m., Marshals De Saxe and Lowendahl and their staffs, with an escort of dragoons and uhlans of De Saxe's corps, arrived at the Brussels Gate. With the thundering of the guns and the chimes of the church bells, they were greeted by the magistrates. Whilst De Saxe and Lowendahl were at the Sint Servaes Church, where a Te Deum was held, their hungry soldiers began plundering the food supplies, which the Allied troops had left behind. 300 French deserters, who had been taken from among the Allied troops when they marched out, were dealt with in the following days. The inhabitants were only grateful the town had not been stormed and ransacked like Bergen op Zoom.

Several days later, the Russian contingent under Prince Repnin reached the Rhine after a lengthy march from Livonia through Bohemia and Germany, only to find out Maastricht had surrendered and hostilities had ended. Repnin was just in time to take part in the peace negotiations in Aix-la-Chapelle.

Aftermath

On 11 May, The French, British and Dutch agreed upon a demilitarised zone, which would keep both parties separated. The Allied front line ran from Steenbergen, Roosendaal, Hoogstraten, Mol, Peer, Bree, to Maaseik, and across the Meuse along the Rur; that of the French from Bergen op Zoom, Putte, Schoten, and Lier, then along the Grote Nete and the Demer, until the Meuse at Rekem. When Austria signed the peace treaty by the end of May, the war in the Austrian Netherlands was over. After the ratification on 18 October 1748, celebrations were held throughout the Republic, although there was little to celebrate in the end. The British demanded that Cronström be tried for his conduct during and after the siege of Bergen op Zoom. Reluctantly, Willem IV had ordered the Extraordinary Military High Court in March 1748 to launch an investigation into the affair. Cronström, eager to have his name cleared, pleaded the High Court several times to give a verdict. It never came. Cronström died in 1751.

Meanwhile, General Schlippenbach noticed how after the armistice the court in The Hague rapidly filled with officers and generals, all seeking promotions and commissions. In order to 'get a piece of the cake', he visited the Stadtholder himself. He was given command of Fort Lillo and three neighbouring fortresses in Zeeland, although his poor health prevented him from living there. He sold his commissions as *inhaber* of his regiment and captain of the elite company, and was awarded a colonel's pension in 1750; the regiment would be dissolved two years later. After falling out of favour, and feeling alienated in court, he finally left The Hague, settling for the quiet life in the country. There, he lived on a meagre income, until he died of a gunshot wound in 1755. His death was ruled a suicide, but it is highly likely he was murdered; who did it, and why, will remain a mystery.

The army, rapidly expanded in the last year, was to be reduced again. Regiments like that of Count Totleben were found to be in a sorry state, and these were the first to be disbanded in the coming year. Despite his scheming, Totleben was awarded a colonel's pension. He was put on a wanted list after eloping with a fifteen year old heiress to a wealthy family – an episode which reads like an adventure novel, with the lovers crossing the Rhine four times to elude anyone chasing them –and in the end, he fled to Prussia. After falling out of favour there, and roaming around again, he finally managed to obtain a commission in the Russian army (having presented a falsified service record). Surprisingly, he was a very successful light troop commander, his greatest feat being the occupation of Berlin in 1760. After fighting in the Russo-

Turkish War (1768–1774), where he made a failed attempt to overthrow the government of Russia's ally Georgia, he was sent to Poland in 1772. He died in Warsaw that same year.

Those surrounding the Stadtholder were worried about his ill health. The birth of a Hereditary Prince of Orange on 8 March 1748 had secured the position of the Orange-Nassau dynasty, but the army needed to be reorganised, which called for a strong and experienced commander. Since Willem IV had refused to give in to any Austrian demands regarding the Barrier Treaty, the relationship between the Republic and Austria had deteriorated quickly, and Bentinck tried his utmost to bring both together again. When in Vienna, Bentinck offered the Duke of Braunschweig-Lüneburg-Bevern the post of commander-in-chief of the Republic's forces; also, if needed, he could aid Princess Anna with the affairs of state (which she already had taken over from her husband), as well as with the education of the prince. The Duke accepted the offer and arrived at court in November 1750, assuming command of the army as field marshal. Willem IV died on 22 October 1751, still rather unexpectedly, at the age of 40. The Duke, better known in the Republic as *Brunswijk* [Brunswick]-Wolfenbüttel, was appointed captain-general. Princess Anna became regent to the young Prince Willem V.

The burial of Willem IV would take place on 4 February 1752. That morning, the drummers of the militia of The Hague struck Assembly at 7:00 a.m., followed by Roll Call half an hour later. The 'Green', *Colombyne*, 'White', 'Orange', 'Blue' and *Oranje Blanche & Bleu* companies took up their positions along the route, the rank and file in either their uniform (if they had it), or otherwise with black waistcoat, breeches, stockings and gloves. At 9:00 a.m., the funeral procession commenced their march through The Hague on their way to Delft. Lieutenant Colonel Nusler, Major of the Court, led the procession, accompanied by a number of sergeants of the ordinance. Then followed the Guard Dragoons, the Horse Guards, the Swiss Guards, the Dutch Guards, and the *Cent Suisses*, all in full dress, followed by the officers of the army and navy present, positioned by rank and age, dressed in their uniform coats, with black waistcoat, breeches, stockings, shoe buckles and gloves, and a black band on the left arm. Everyone wore orange cockades. The household of the Stadtholder, all dressed in black robes, followed after that, from the stewards, valets, and his black servant Jean Rabo, to the pastry chefs, the dancing master, and the apothecary. Then came the parade of horses, banners and standards, all the symbols of power, the crown, and the members of several councils; and in between heralds, kettledrummers and trumpeters. Then came the carriage, drawn by eight horses, led by two lieutenant colonels and six majors of the cavalry; on it, the body of the Stadtholder was laid in a gilded lead coffin. Marshal Van Nassau-Ouwerkerk, General Praetorius, and Lieutenant-Admirals of the Navy Schrijver and Reynst each held a corner of the pall, whilst the corps was carried by 22 major generals and two rear admirals; above it was a canopy, held up by 23 colonels. The carriage was escorted by four *sous-brigadiers* of the *Guarde du Corps*, and followed by two sergeants of the ordinance, of the Swiss and Dutch Guards. Behind the carriage came the deputies of the States General and the States of Holland, the high council of Holland, Zeeland, and Friesland, the presidents and councils of justice, and finally the magistrates and ministers of The Hague and Delft. As the procession slowly made its way through The Hague, the militia presented arms until the last magistrate had passed. The procession then moved to Delft; the whole was escorted by a detachment of four officers, two NCOs and 80 troopers of the *Guarde du Corps*, who remained with the carriage until the procession arrived at the gate. After a slow march through Delft, the procession finally reached the Nieuwe Kerk at the Grote Markt, where the *Guarde du Corps* and the *Cent Suisses* formed up at the entrance of the church, whilst the other regiments marched back to The Hague. The militia of Delft, with black cloth around their hats, sashes, and pole arms, formed up on three sides of the Grote Markt, whilst a battery of 21 guns fired a volley when the body of the Stadtholder was carried into the church, and again when it was lowered into the vault. After a long day of ceremonies, the Stadtholder was at his final resting place, and the troops back in their garrison.

Continuation of the Old System

With the ratification of the peace of Aix-la-Chapelle, the question was now to whom the Barrier towns would be handed over: according to article six, the towns should be handed over to the Republic. Britain supported this wholeheartedly. The French, who had largely demolished the defensive works of the barrier towns in the Austrian Netherlands, also had no objections. When the Republic had sent troops to man the garrisons again, engineers immediately investigated the state of these defences: they reported that the defences of Menin had been completely dismantled; the citadel of Tournay had been heavily damaged, as had the defences of Ypres; those of Veurne, Knokke, and Namur were slightly damaged. The total cost for repairing and rebuilding these would be around 1.7 million guilders. Also, the Austrian strongholds of Oudenaarde, Ath, Charleroi, and Mons had been demolished. According to the Republic, the rebuilding and maintaining of the Barrier Towns and fortresses was a matter for the Sea Powers and Austria, and all had to share in the costs. However, the Dutch and British envoys were faced with an Austrian diplomat who had no intention of enforcing the Barrier Treaty: Wenzel Anton Count Kaunitz-Rietberg (1711–1794). According to him, Prussia formed the real threat to Austria, not France, and the old alliance and system had made the emergence of that new power possible: had Austria not lost Silesia because it had been fighting France in the Netherlands? Furthermore, why pay millions of subsidies again, when the Barrier had been dismantled, and there was no Barrier to talk about in the first place? What was more, there were no subsidies available, since the Austrian Netherlands had been bled dry. The Barrier Treaty had become powerless and impractical, and therefore obsolete. To counter the Prussian threat, Austria had signed a treaty with Russia.

The question was whether the Republic was powerful enough still to maintain its position as it had done before the war. The Dutch feared the Austrians would demand a lift on the trade restrictions, such as a lift on the ban on the Oostende Company, in return for their continuance of the Barrier Treaty. The Stadtholder, the Council of State, and the States General were unwilling to give in to any Austrian demands regarding the trade: it would mean the acknowledgement of the idea that the Barrier Treaty was obsolete. In a resolution of 27 August 1749, they demanded Austria would pay the required subsidies for the Republic to maintain a force in the Austrian Netherlands – even though the subsidies would not suffice to pay for even half of the 12,000 men needed – or otherwise, the Republic felt it was no longer required to do so. This would end the alliance between Austria and the Sea Powers, as Austria would then have to defend her Netherlands territories herself. However, with the Barrier towns in ruins the Republic had nothing to offer, and it needed British support to convince the Austrians to re-establish the Barrier Treaty. For Britain, it was clear that France and Prussia had to be kept in check, in order to maintain peace and stability in Europe. The threat that the Republic would step out of the Barrier Treaty and opt for neutrality in the future, which it had protested against strongly in 1745 and 1746, was most unwelcome.

On 20 December, the Austrians answered that there could be no subsidy, since Austria needed the money to maintain a 25,000 strong army in the Austrian Netherlands, roughly 8,000 more than stipulated in the Barrier Treaty in the first place. In order to come to an agreement, it asked the Sea Powers if they wanted to strictly hold Austria to the terms of the Barrier Treaty, thus having her pay the subsidies in full, or if they were willing to discuss other means of military cooperation. This was unacceptable, since that would acknowledge the Austrian stance on the Barrier, but convincing the Austrians of the necessity of rebuilding the Barrier, and together maintain a force of 30- to 40,000 men, would mean entering new trade negotiations. In January 1750, Austria and the Republic had still not come to an agreement. It was offered to not have to pay any behind payments on the subsidies from the years 1744–1748, and a lowering of the total subsidy, but on the condition that all payments were made in time from then on. In return, the Republic would give in to some of the demands of the Austrian Netherlands regarding trade, if they would not harm or interfere with the trade of the Sea Powers. Austria refused. Bentinck had travelled to Vienna to re-establish the ties between Austria and the Republic. After almost a year, he returned to the Republic in August; the only goal he had achieved was that the Duke of Brunswick came to the Republic to assume command. To his surprise he learned that the Stadtholder had demanded that Britain would pay for the rebuilding of the Barrier towns, before there could be talk of joining the Austro-Russian alliance. He had received a letter, which read that Britain was not willing to give in to blackmail: 'it will never be admitted as a consequence, that, if England does not contribute 50,000 Pounds [...] the Barrier is to be abandoned and the Republic flung into the arms of France.' According to the Barrier Treaty, Britain only supported the Barrier with troops, as it had done in the last war. Willem IV went against the advice of his council in this: he was not willing to start any rebuilding of the Barrier before financial support from Britain was secure. According to him, the Republic had given in too much already into the British demands, and taking a step back would be a good idea.

Deadlock

A new offer was made to Austria in the resolution of 27 August 1751: a new trade agreement would be signed if Austria would start paying back its debts, half a million in advance, and then 60,000 every month, to support the rebuilding of the Barrier. Bentinck wrote to his British colleagues that it was in both their interests to agree with this resolution, since the safety and trade interests of the Sea Powers were under threat: instead of rebuilding the defences, the money sent to the Austrian Netherlands was used to finance canals, in order to improve trade routes. However, the British only repeated their promise of military support in the future. Austria answered on January 13 1752 that it would only start paying after a new trade agreement was signed. Princess Anna, who despised Bentinck, was determined not to give in; there was now a real threat that the Republic would withdraw its troops from the Austrian Netherlands. A letter from Austrian Lieutenant General Henrici von Calenberg to a member of the British Parliament illustrated the Austrian sentiments: it suggested that the fortresses and towns had been easily captured by the French in 1744 to 1746, because the governors and commanders had failed to do their duty, and perhaps even had made a deal with the French. In short, the Republic might not even have the right to demand payments, since they were themselves to blame for the loss of the towns during the war. Furthermore, since Austria was willing to defend the Netherlands herself, and the Republic was safe behind her own Water Line and defences, there was no more need for a Barrier Treaty.

Britain was worried about the uncompromising stances of Austria and the Republic: she had welcomed the Austro-Russian alliance, since Russia would make a welcome addition to the existing alliance between the Sea Powers and Austria; but if the Republic remained neutral, let alone if she sided with the French, that meant Britain would have no more foothold in Europe. At the conference in Brussels, which opened on 4 May 1752, she made it clear there could be no alliance with Austria without the Republic, and that Austria had to pay up. Austria answered that, since the Republic had proven unable to defend the Austrian Netherlands, she would do it herself; payments would be made after a new trade agreement was signed, and if Britain would also finance the rebuilding of the Barrier towns.

Kaunitz contacted Bentinck to try and resolve the differences. They met in Brussels in January, where Kaunitz handed him a proposal, containing five articles: 1) Austria demanded a new, trade agreement; 2) Maria Theresia would in the meantime take unilateral trade measures, within the limits of former treaties; 3) after the convention was signed, Austria would resume paying the subsidies; in return, the Republic would give up on the overdue subsidy payments; 4) the Republic would accept only a third of the subsidies, since the other two thirds were to be used for rebuilding the Barrier towns and for the 25,000 Austrian troops; 5) all parties would do their utmost to maintain peace and stability in Europe, and guarantee each other's safety. Despite Bentincks' support for the proposal, he returned from The Hague in February with instructions to rejects articles 1, 3 and 5: article 1 was contradictory to the articles of the Barrier Treaty; article 3 was out of the question, since Austria owed the Republic over 7 million guilders; and article

5 could not be agreed upon since the Republic had already committed itself to this through the Barrier Treaty. There was reason to believe Austria would try and recapture Silesia, once it had assured itself of enough military support from the Sea Powers to keep France at bay, as the French would undoubtedly come to Prussia's aid. Bentinck could not reach an agreement with Kaunitz in the months that followed. Kaunitz finally left Brussels and assumed the position of *Hofkanzler* in Vienna.

Bentinck gained some support for his idea that the Republic should show some leniency towards Austria regarding a new trade agreement and the payment of the overdue subsidies; Britain supported him in this, knowing full well that in order to save the old alliance and British interests, the Republic had to be compensated one way or the other. Together, the British and Dutch envoys in Vienna offered a counterproposal in March 1754, demanding half of the overdue subsidies. Kaunitz warned Bentinck in private that this would be unacceptable for Maria Theresia. He gave the official answer in June: Austria rejected the counterproposal. A second counterproposal was also rejected: if there was to be no new trade agreement, no subsidies would be paid. It had been almost seven years now since the Peace of Aix-la-Chapelle was signed, and the Barrier towns had still not been rebuilt.

3

A Second Rate Power

The Expeditionary Force to Suriname

The Republic had numerous colonies in the East- and West Indies and Africa, which were run by private corporations like the United East India Company (VOC) and the West India Company (WIC). The VOC had its own army and fleet, which, with the aid of allied local sultanates and kingdoms, fought against competing East India companies. The West India Company organised local militias, aimed mainly at keeping the peace. There had been numerous slave revolts in the West Indian colonies throughout the 17th and 18th centuries. Usually, these revolts occurred on one plantation, where the slaves would refuse to go to work and run away; sometimes they obtained weapons, killed their masters, and either fled or attacked other plantations. In Suriname, the greatest threat came from the *Marrons*. These were tribes that originated from runaway African slaves who had retreated deep into the jungle. Their settlements were fortified villages, often located in swamps, from where they would launch raids against the plantations to obtain weapons, tools, provisions and women. The *Sociëteit van Suriname* (Society of Suriname), a private company owned by the WIC, the city of Amsterdam, and the Van Aerssen van Sommelsdijk family, was responsible for the defence of the colony. It had organised a militia, which, with the help from armed civilian volunteers and slaves, would go on expeditions to hunt down the *Marrons*. This militia was paid for by the Republic since 1683, when the *Sociëteit* had signed agreements with all the separate provinces to have on the muster roll of every company on their establishment (except those of the Swiss and Guard regiments) a 'man for Suriname': this meant one soldier was absent, while the funds for his payment were paid to the *Sociëteit*. This system was used by practically all regiments as a means to pay off debts.

The expeditions had little, or only temporary success; most slave revolts were easily put down, but if any of the *Marron* tribes were involved, the colony was under serious threat. In March 1750, news reached the Republic that a detachment of 100 men from the militia, with 400 volunteers, had successfully attacked a force of 5,500 rebels and forced them to sign a peace agreement. In reality, an agreement had been signed with a band of 1,600 runaway slaves on 20 September 1749, but the revolt soon spiralled out of control. There were numerous raids on plantations, and the *Sociëteit* reluctantly had to send the States General an urgent request for military aid.

In May, an order was sent to 41 battalions to send one sergeant and one corporal each; 20 other battalions were ordered to each send one drummer and one corporal. All companies – except those of the Guard and Swiss regiments – received the order to send one private. From these troops, a regiment of 10 companies was organised in Willemstad, consisting of 21 sergeants, 31 corporals, 10 drummers and 328 privates; a reserve corps of 20 sergeants, 30 corporals, 10 drummers and 290 privates was organised in Naarden. Each company would consist of one captain, one lieutenant (or a captain-lieutenant in the life guard- and colonel-commanders' companies), one 2nd lieutenant, one ensign, two sergeants, three corporals, one drummer, one *schrijver* (secretary or paymaster), and 29 privates. The captains and subalterns were to be recruited from the officers on half pay or pensions. The staff consisted of Major General (also Colonel) Baron Spörcke, Adjutant-General Cronsaz, Lieutenant Colonel Baron Verschuer, Major De Bermond, an adjutant, and Surgeon-Major Mester and three surgeons. The whole was paid for by the Republic, although the officers and men would receive their pay and their provisions from the *Sociëteit*. The regiment was embarked on four ships, which sailed from Texel on 10 September 1750.

Upon arrival, Major General Spörcke found a colony in turmoil: Governor Mauricius was opposed by rich planter families in the colonies, the latter sending accusations against him to the States General. Spörcke took over temporarily while Mauricius resigned and travelled to the Republic to plead his case. Unfortunately Spörcke died in 1752, and Princess Anna and Brunswick-Wolfenbüttel had to intervene in the affair regarding the appointment of a new governor. Meanwhile, the troops fought their way through the jungle against an invisible foe. They managed to drive the rebels away from the plantations and restore order, but this was only temporary. There were to be 15 slave revolts between 1750 and 1759; peace treaties were then signed with the largest *Marron* tribes, the Ndyuka (1760), Saamaka (1762), and Matawai (1767). These treaties guaranteed their independent status and gave them territorial rights, in return for no involvement in, or support for, future revolts.

The Reorganisation of the Army

During the final year of the War of the Austrian Succession, the army had consisted of 126 battalions and 84 squadrons. After the war, it was once again drastically reduced. Several of the new regiments were immediately disbanded in 1749, given the state these were in. The strength of the peacetime army was set on 38,000 men, including 10,000 Swiss troops; in reality, the number was no more than 33,000 men. In January, 1752, the army was further reduced by 2,000 men, by disbanding one Swiss regiment, the Regiment of French Grenadiers, the *Jager* Corps, and the State Hussars. Despite its small numbers, maintaining the army was still a costly affair, with regiments being undermanned, especially in the infantry: almost all regiments consisted of one battalion, but had – at least on paper – a complete regimental staff and an officer corps to match. On 2 March 1752, the resolution regarding the 'Plan of Incorporation of the Troops of this Republic', drawn up in sixteen articles, passed the States General:

Article I: Since the number of troops had already been reduced to a bare minimum, it was clear that another reduction in numbers would have no effect. The solution was therefore to reduce the number of companies, and reorganise the regiments, in order to make the army more cost effective.

Article II: The cavalry, consisting of one regiment of Horse Guards and 12 line regiments, all of six companies, were to be reduced to one regiment of Horse Guards of six companies, and six line cavalry regiments of eight companies each. This was done by having two companies amalgamated with the other four, and then combining two regiments into one. Six regimental staffs were therefore dissolved, as were 24 companies.

Article III: The dragoons consisted of one regiment of Guard Dragoons and three line regiments, each of nine companies. The four regiments were to be reorganised into three regiments of eight companies each, making four squadrons, like the cavalry. Two companies of the Guard Dragoons were to be amalgamated with the other eight. Three companies in Trips' Regiment were amalgamated with the remaining six, whilst in Massau's and Ditfourth's, four companies were to be amalgamated with the remaining five; the companies of Ditfourth's would then be divided amongst Trips' and Massau's Regiments. One regimental staff and 13 companies were dissolved.

Article IV: The National and German infantry numbered 48 regiments; 44 or those consisted of one battalion of 10 companies, three regiments (*Oranje-Gelderland*, *Oranje-Stad en Lande* and Baden-Baden) consisted of one battalion of 12 companies, and one regiment (*Oranje-Friesland*) of 24 companies, organised into two battalions. The grand total of 500 National and German companies were to be reorganised into 25 regiments, each of two battalions, each battalion of seven companies (six musketeers and one grenadier). There were four Scots Regiments, three of two battalions and one of one battalion, each battalion having 10 companies; these 70 companies were to be reorganised into three regiments, like the National and German regiments. Finally, there were three Walloon regiments, each of one battalion of 10 companies; the 30 companies were to be organised into one regiment of three battalions, each of seven companies. This meant a reduction of 187 companies in total.

Article V: All NCO's, trumpeters, drummers and privates who would become redundant would either be transferred to other units, or discharged. No musicians were to be kept with the regiments, unless paid for by the officers themselves. All privates that were to be transferred to other companies, would do so with their uniforms, accoutrements and weapons; the troopers and dragoons taking their horses also with them. Colonels would have to send lists of redundant personnel to the States General, so that it was decided who would be transferred to other regiments, and who would be sent away on half pay.

Article VI: When in effect, the army would consist of:

Cavalry	2,106
Dragoons	936
National and German troops	17,000
Scots	2,040
Walloon	1,020
Total	**23,102**

It was acknowledged that this number (to which five Swiss regiments were to be added) was very low, 'considering the situation of the Republic', and it was stressed that the units had to be maintained up to strength at all times. As mentioned in Article V, the whole project would have to be finished on 24 March, the new organisation going into effect on 25 March.

Article VII: The reorganisation of the regiments meant that kettledrummers, drum majors, regimental *picqeurs*, adjutants, surgeons, etc. were now official ranks within the regiments, and thus the pay for each company was officially established. Also, corporals, grenadiers, and grenadier drummers received a raise.

Articles VIII and IX dealt with the debts of the regiments, and how these were resolved, while articles X and XI were about the payment of pensions and half-pay for the officers which were now discharged from their positions. Articles XII to XV specified reductions in the regiments of Saxe-Gotha, the Swiss regiments, the artillery, and sappers and miners respectively. In conclusion, article XVI summed up the reorganisation, and gave lists of the composition and pay of each company.

To improve uniformity within the army, a resolution regarding the clothing of the army was passed in May 1752: the cavalry regiments were to be dressed in white from now on, except the Horse Guards; the dragoons kept their blue uniforms; and all infantry was to be dressed in blue, except the Scots regiments, which kept their distinctive red uniforms. The *inhabers* of the regiments retained the right to choose the colours of the facings and smallclothes as they pleased. The officers, 'from the colonel, to the ensign' were to appear in court only in their full regimentals. Just as in earlier regulations, it was again stressed that it was strictly forbidden to have any gold or silver lace and/or embroidery on the coats and waistcoats of the officers (except those of the guard units), nor have the buttonholes worked with gold or silver thread. Gold and silver decoration was only allowed on the hats, the design of which was left up to the preference of the *inhaber*.

Given the experiences in the War of the Austrian Succession, a new exercise for the infantry was adopted in 1749, based on the Prussian exercise. That same year, the Stadtholder instructed Marshal Nassau-Ouwerkerk to discuss a new system for the cavalry and dragoons with the cavalry generals. Schlippenbach, as Lieutenant General, took part in the meeting:

> For five hours, nothing else was done but going through exercise books, especially those of Major General Bland, which the marshal was very fond of, and whose system he wanted to adopt. When the time was up, we had to leave and set a new date. During this time, we spoke. Everybody did his utmost to elaborate on his method and convince us of it, but the opinions differed so much, that no decision could be made. General Trips stated that, since H.S.H. had approved of the Prussian exercise for the infantry, he would also approve of an adaptation of that of the cavalry. This proposal was not accepted, but no one came up with good arguments to contradict this. [...] After a lot of talking back and forth, it was decided that every general and Lieutenant General would give a presentation about a method of exercise to his own insight. All plans would be evaluated then, and from every project would be selected that which was suitable for application in general.

Schlippenbach worked for 13 days, drawing up a method based on the Prussian system. He had two copies made, one bound in calfskin and sent to the Stadtholder, 'so that this gentleman would know it was not my fault that his order had not yet been executed', the other sent to Nassau-Ouwerkerk. Schlippenbach learned that the Stadtholder was pleased with his work, but that was all, and the generals apparently never met anymore. Five years later, the 1754 regulations for the manual exercise and movements of the cavalry and dragoons were published.

Renversement des Alliances

In the background, tensions grew between France and Britain, as, in North America, the hostilities between French and British colonials increased. It would be a matter of time before these skirmishes would result in war in Europe. The Republic might have to send another auxiliary corps to Britain: with the Barrier towns still in ruins, there was no doubt that any support for Britain would result in a quick advance of the French army through the Netherlands, where it could strike directly at the heart of the Republic. In June 1755, Brunswick-Wolfenbüttel argued for an immediate augmentation of the army with 13,500 men, which Princess Anna proposed to the States General. The debate that followed was almost a replay of the endless bickering of the early years of the War of the Austrian Succession: Dordrecht objected, with support of Amsterdam, Rotterdam and Haarlem, and instead opted for neutrality. To the horror of Bentinck, Anna, and Brunswick-Wolfenbüttel, the States of Holland proposed to ask the French what their plans were for the Austrian Netherlands in the coming conflict. With the proposal came a guarantee by the French ambassador that France was willing to negotiate the Republic's neutrality, since Louis XV did not want to 'multiply his enemies, and do his utmost not to have the "quarrels" with Britain result in an all-out war'. Despite Anna forcing Gelderland, Utrecht, Stad en Lande, and Overijssel to vote against the proposal, and the Republic thus not entering negotiations with France, there would be no augmentation, since Holland, Zeeland, and

Friesland, who paid for most of the army, were unwilling to finance it. And on top of that, Anna was told by her father George II that Britain would not send troops to Europe, since the coming war would only be a naval conflict, thus enabling her to make whatever treaty with the French she would like. Britain did however demand that the Republic would send an auxiliary corps if the French invaded Britain. Meanwhile, France put the Republic under pressure, urging her to state what she would do once war would break out. So in January 1756, the States General announced that the Republic would stay out of the conflict since it was promised that the Austrian Netherlands and the Republic itself would not be invaded; but that it would come to the aid of Britain if there was to be an invasion of the British Isles or in Ireland.

Within a fortnight, this announcement was made completely ineffective by the Treaty of Westminster between Prussia and Britain on 16 January; in it, both agreed to stay out of each other's German territories. Britain was assured that Hannover was now safe from both France and Prussia. To put more pressure on the Republic, a transport fleet arrived in March to pick up the auxiliary corps; if no troops would be sent, and the Republic thus chose to remain neutral, then Britain was free to attack Dutch merchant vessels. Bentinck proposed a compromise: in exchange for the auxiliary corps, Britain would mobilise a Hanoverian corps of 10,000 men to protect the Republic, and she would agree not to attack any Dutch merchant ships. Dordrecht however, said the Republic had to choose the lesser of two evils: rather have the British do damage to Dutch trade, than be dragged into a war with France. Haarlem reminded the States of Holland of how Britain had abandoned the Republic in 1745 and 1746. Also, it did not expect Austria would want to be part of a conflict over British possessions in North America. Amsterdam and Rotterdam supported Dordrecht and Haarlem, and thus no auxiliary corps was sent to Britain.

The Council of Haarlem had been right all along: already in 1755, Austria had decided to remain neutral in the conflict between Britain and France over their overseas colonies, even if it meant that France would occupy the Austrian Netherlands. Also, the British-Prussian alliance had come as no surprise. Instead, as Kaunitz had predicted, France approached Austria. The time had come to exchange the Old System for a New System of a Catholic alliance against a Protestant alliance. After the decision was made in March 1756 to abandon the Old System, Austria and France signed the Treaty of Versailles on 1 May, thereby guaranteeing to come to each other's aid when attacked by one of Britain's allies. France acknowledged the neutrality of the Austrian Netherlands and Liege. After that, Britain declared war on France on 17 May. Eight days later, the States General declared it would remain neutral. War erupted once again when Prussian troops invade Saxony on August 29. The *Renversement des Alliances* brought the Old System to an end. Bentinck could not believe it, but Austria had tossed the Barrier Treaty aside and lost all interest in the Netherlands: with the second Treaty of Versailles, Maria Theresia granted France the towns of Oostende, Nieuwport, Mons, Chimay, Beaumont, and the Barrier towns of Veurne, Knokke, and Ypres, if Silesia was recaptured; the rest would be exchanged with the Duke of Parma for his Italian possessions.

With the destruction of the Barrier towns, and the Old Alliance dissolved, the Republic had lost her status as one of the great European powers. What lay ahead was strict neutrality, whilst Britain and France fought over their overseas possessions. With her fleet and army in decline, the Republic was no longer a serious competitor against both these colonial powers.

The Seven Years War

In an answer to the Republic's declaration of neutrality of 25 May, King Louis XV had proclaimed on 14 June that this neutrality would be honoured by the French, and that the territories of the Republic would not be invaded. Indeed, they were doing their utmost to keep away from the border. To make sure no mistakes were made, the borders were marked with signs, and guides were provided to the French armies. The French occupation of Oostende and Nieuwpoort was perhaps worrying, but the French were being as tactful as possible. Besides, the Republic could not expect the French to remain outside the Austrian Netherlands, since the French and Austrians were now allies. In the territories around Staats Opper-Gelre, the geographical locations of the borders were alas unclear, and a French army mistakenly entered Dutch territory, for which they offered their most sincere apologies. This happened again when a Prussian-Hanoverian army commanded by Ferdinand of Brunswick, *en route* after the Battle of Krefeld (23 June 1758), marched into the same area; Ferdinand answered to the States' protests that he could have avoided making this mistake if he had been assisted by the same guides who had previously aided the French.

Tensions grew between the Republic and Britain, as British ships began capturing Dutch merchant vessels: already in the summer of 1756, a convoy, escorted by a single man-of-war, was seized by a British force. Since the ships were laden with goods that were not prohibited by any agreement, the Dutch ambassador protested against their capture. Also, fear of yet another Jacobite invasion made trade with the French suspect, for instance when 80 small draft ships were hired in Amsterdam: officially for the salt trade, but, it was feared, these might just be used to transport troops across the Channel. Thus Parliament sought a means of limiting the trade between the Dutch merchants and France as much as possible, arguing that remaining neutral in trading was virtually impossible: carrying French goods as a neutral party meant involvement in the war. And the duty to remain completely impartial outweighed the right of being a 'privileged neutral'; Dutch trade with the French meant the Republic would be more beneficial to France as a neutral than as an ally, it was said, and the rule of 'free ships – free goods' meant difficulties in trying to end that trade.

Smuggling between the French and Dutch colonies in the West Indies was impossible to prevent, but since it was common knowledge that most – if not all – trade from Curaçao and St. Eustatius was illegal (or at least highly suspect), the British fleet began capturing Dutch merchant ships when they came out of French ports, and even when they left Dutch ports. This led to a storm of protests, not only from the captains and masters of the vessels themselves, but also from the Dutch merchants, especially those from Amsterdam, who requested several times that Princess Anna and the

States General would protest against these attacks. Princess Anna indeed sent protests, but she received British complaints in return. At home, she was caught between the Orangist and Republican factions: the first argued for an augmentation of the army, while the latter, always the Anglophobes, argued that the fleet needed to be strengthened to withstand the attacks on merchant ships by British naval vessels and privateers. On 7 December 1758, the Amsterdam merchants, for the fourth time, handed an address to the princess. In it, they urged again for expansion of the fleet, and demanded that emissaries would be sent to the British court and those of other neutral states. To Anna's dismay, they had already printed and distributed the address throughout Holland before they had had their audience. The princess answered that she was not to blame for the sorry state of the army and fleet, and that she would do her utmost for the trade interests of the Republic. Four days later, she made her final address to the States General, proposing to expand the army and the fleet, and expressing her anger over the merchants' impertinence. It was clear the pressure of the protests and the strong division in the Republic began to take its toll on her. On 12 January 1759, Anna, the 'Governess of the Republic', died; she was buried on 23 February in the Nieuwe Kerk in Delft.

There was no augmentation of the army; for any aspiring officer, the States' army had little to offer. It was expected, certainly by its officers and the rank and file, that at least the Scots Brigade would be recalled to Britain. Instead, recruiting in Britain was suspended as of 1757; the regiments now had to recruit in the Republic and elsewhere to fill the ranks. An Act of Parliament was passed on 31 March 1756, in which the officers were obliged 'to take and subscribe the Oaths of Allegiance and Abjuration' like their colleagues in Britain, something which had never been necessary before. Despite the Brigade being ready to be deployed, it seemed that Britain chose instead to raise new regiments for the duration of the war. Rumour had it that Princess Anna had requested her father King George II to keep the Scots Brigade in the Republic, to protect the young Prince of Orange against the Republican factions, which were suspected to be under French influence. It was now clear that the Brigade would not be recalled, and the officers and men were devastated.

The Secretary of State to King George II, Robert Darcy Earl of Holdernesse (1718–1778), wrote a proposal on 16 June 1758 to Brunswick-Wolfenbüttel on returning part of the Scots Brigade to Britain:

> The Scots Brigade numbering strictly only three effective battalions, yet has the officers for six battalions; and this corps will not be able to exist for a long time, if a solution to remove the obstacles that prevent us from recruiting as usual can be found. We therefore propose to remedy the known inconveniences thusly:
>
> > *Primo*. That from now on the Scots Brigade in service of the States, will consist of three battalions of nine companies each.
> > *2do*. That from the officers presently there, the King will choose as much as needed to provide three battalions of nine companies each, at His service.

> That the Scots Corps will also provide the sergeants of 27 companies, which will immediately enter the service of the King.
>
> *3o.* That a new capitulation will be made for the three Battalions which must remain in the service of the Republic, of which the main articles will be:
>
> I. That the King will appoint the officers of the Staff of the said Corps.
>
> II. That all officers will swear to His Majesty the oaths accustomed, as well as that of fidelity to the States General.
>
> III. We will give permission to recruit a number of men every year to complete this Corps.
>
> IV. The Scots Brigade will keep the rank it currently has among the troops of the Republic.
>
> V. In case of an attack on His Majesty's possessions, He may recall this Corps to its service, and to render it as much as possible up to the strength of the English troops.
>
> VI. It will be at the disposal of the Republic everywhere in Europe, but cannot be sent to the Overseas Colonies.
>
> VII. Some arrangement will be needed in relation to the Council of War and the administration of justice in this Corps.

Included with this proposal was a proposal of a Captain William Greeme of Colyear's Regiment, to 'raise a new regiment of Scots of ten or twelve companies, without any expense to the Republic further than the loans which would take effect on the same day as the other new levies would receive them'. Even King George II requested in a letter dated 30 October 1759 that half of the Brigade would be sent to Germany and join the command of Prince Ferdinand of Brunswick-Wolfenbüttel, the Duke's younger brother. But Brunswick-Wolfenbüttel declined and the Brigade never saw any action. In July 1763, the British Secretary of War received 'A memorial of the commanding officers of the Scots Brigade in the Dutch service, in behalf of the said troops and their officers', in which they expressed their desire to be removed from Dutch service, since:

> ...they can find in their own hearts no consciousness of any reason why they should be suffered to languish in a foreign country rather than to be restored to a proper establishment suitable to the rank of 'Royal British auxiliaries', or be employed by their native Sovereign against his enemies, and in preserving and vindicating the rights of the British nation.

It was of no avail. Orders for recruiting in Scotland were given the year after, only to be withdrawn again shortly afterwards. The ranks would now be slowly filling with non-Scots recruits in the years to come.

The Republic benefited somewhat financially from neutrality: the inhabitants had not only been spared the taxation and debt for financing the war, but several old debts had been payed off, and international trade albeit shameless war profiteering – had flourished, since French and allied armies had been supplied by Dutch merchants, such as Leendert Pieter de Neufville, a merchant banker who sold gunpowder, supplies, and uniforms to Prussia. The Dutch investments in French and, especially, British funds had been profitable. Speculation and a booming trade in bills of exchange and letters of credit ultimately led to an international banking crisis after the Peace of Hubertusburg, but despite some bankruptcies in Amsterdam, the Republic came out of the crash of 1763 unscathed. However, over 135 merchant ships had been captured, most in the West Indies, which amounted to a substantial financial loss. Britain had gained much from the Treaty of Paris: besides the exchange of colonial territories, the French were also forced to demolish the fortifications of Dunkirk, from which the British always feared an invasion could be launched. Meanwhile, the Treaty of Hubertusburg meant Austria reluctantly kept her Netherlands territories.

The Berbice Slave Revolt

Berbice was the second most profitable colony in the Americas, after Suriname. It was privately owned by five families, who bought it in 1720. These families then founded the *Sociëteit van Berbice,* which was modelled after the *Sociëteit van Suriname,* to govern the colony. On 23 February 1763 a slave revolt broke out at the Magdalenberg Plantation. The slaves burned down the plantation, acquired muskets and ammunition, and continued to liberate more slaves at other plantations. A man named Cuffy or Kofi assumed leadership over the rebel army, which grew to number about 2,500–3,000 men. The colonists, outnumbered and unable to counter the guerrilla tactics of the rebel army, fled to the coastal areas up north, where they dug in and barely held off several attacks. On 2 April Cuffy proposed a peace treaty, whereby the colony would be divided up between the colonists and the slaves. When he received no answer, he ordered an attack on 13 May, which was repelled with great losses. The war thus dragged on, in which the rebels often clashed with war parties of the Carib and Akowaio tribes and Creoles, allied to the Dutch. No offensive was organised by the colonists, since the rainy season had started and most of the 400 militiamen were sick with fevers or dysentery. On 8 June, the Lord Directors of the colony requested the States General to send another two frigates and at least 600 regular troops to help quell the rebellion.

The *Sociëteit* had sent two ships and 50 men in July, followed by three ships and 400 men in August sent by the States General. For the auxiliary force, the Admiralties of the Meuse and Amsterdam would each send a ship, while a regiment was raised for the period of 18 months, commanded by Lieutenant General Jan Marius de Salve (1708–1768). The regiment consisted of two battalions of each six companies, a total of 600 men, with the addition of carpenters, artillerymen and engineers. As suggested by Brunswick-Wolfenbüttel, the officers that volunteered for service were to receive a higher rank than which they had, while the rank and file, a total of 72 NCOs, 468 corporals and privates, 12 drummers, and 40 gunners, were recruited from among volunteers from the infantry regiments. The troops were gathered at Naarden, and from there shipped to Texel. The expeditionary force set sail on November 6 and arrived at Berbice on 26 December.

With the troops of the *Sociëteit,* and those sent by the States General arriving in Berbice, the colonists were confident enough to organise a counterattack in November. A force was gathered for the offensive, consisting of several detachments of the militia, additional troops from the Suriname militia, naval detachments, a British officer and 30 volunteers from neighbouring Essequebo, and Amerindian and Creole guides. The aim was to destroy the crops and fields of the rebels, and occupy the plantations, thereby denying the rebel forces their food supplies. The intention was not to hunt and kill the rebels, but persuade them to give themselves up. A fleet of ships from the *Sociëteit* thus sailed up the river, where detachments would disembark and occupy strategic locations to cut off the rebels' path, or send out patrols. The rebels were driven from the plantations, but it was impossible to pursue them further into the jungle. Rebels who surrendered or defected all told how there was infighting among the rebel army, and that they had little to no food and provisions. After a month of fighting, most soldiers and militiamen were exhausted or ill. Loyal slaves, Creoles, and Amerindians were the only effective troops that patrolled the countryside, looking for any rebel bands left. When De Salve's Regiment finally arrived, it was immediately sent out to man the military posts and relieve the exhausted troops.

Already, after the defeat on 13 May, the position of Cuffy had been challenged by some of his lieutenants. Several groups split off the rebel army, and fought amongst each other. Eventually, Cuffy was defeated by the leader Atta and committed suicide. The rebel army was now dispersed, but although many rebels surrendered, small groups still offered resistance, living in isolated villages which were hard to find, much like the *Marrons* of Suriname. On 23 March 1764, 200 soldiers and armed slaves attacked such a rebel village, located in the middle of a swamp. The group of 200 rebels was defeated, and their leader Accabré surrendered. Being an enemy of Atta, he defected to the Dutch. Atta himself was captured on 14 April by two defected slaves, Accara and Gousarie, and handed over to De Salve. On 27 April, Atta and 31 other rebel leaders were executed publicly. Atta was tied to a stake and tortured for about four hours by ripping away his flesh with red hot pliers every seven to eight minutes, and then slowly burned to death. Five others were also burned alive, eight were broken on the wheel without administering a *coup de grâce*, and 18 were hanged. On 16 June, another 32 rebels were executed; by then, the rebellion had ended. In July and August, the colonists returned to their plantations. On 14 December, the last eight rebel leaders were executed, after which a general pardon was proclaimed.

De Salve's troops had suffered from the harsh climate and diseases: in February, he had 380 men left, but, by the end of July, all officers except De Salve were sick, and there were no more than 20 healthy men left. On 14 August, he expressed his wish to the colonists to return to the Republic, having received orders from Brunswick-Wolfenbüttel to do so if the revolt had ended. By request of the colonists, Major Fourgeoud and 101 volunteers stayed in Berbice. After having to wait for ships (with healthy sailors, since diseases had also decimated the naval personnel), the troops embarked on 2 October. The weather made it almost impossible to reach open sea, which they barely managed on 24 November; heavy wind forced them to sail to Curaçao, which they reached on 4 December. After the ships were repaired and the men regained their health, the troops were embarked again. The ships left on 26 January 1765, only to be dispersed by heavy storms. In April and

Posthumous portrait of Colonel Fourgeoud, commanding the Marine Regiment nr. 21 in Surinam, 1772–1774. Fourgeoud was an experienced and able commander, leading his troops in person. He wears a shortened coat, a leather cap and breeches that button down on the sides. He is armed with his officers' sword, a musket and a pistol – the holster is visible on his left. In the background a column of marines, followed by slaves carrying supplies. (Rijksmuseum)

May, one after another ship arrived at Texel, where the troops were shipped back to their garrison in Naarden.

In Berbice, Fourgeoud and his troops, consisting of two captains, five lieutenants, six NCOs, six corporals, two drummers, 70 privates, eight artillerymen and two surgeons, regained their health; many began working in the colony as craftsmen or on the plantations. The colonists had requested to the Lord Directors of the colony to recruit and send replacements, so that the troops could return. Fourgeoud and his men embarked on 29 March 1765, taking Accara and Gousarie with them. They reached open sea on 24 April. After a stop on St. Eustatius from 6 May to 11 June, they arrived at Texel on 10 August. By order of the States General, De Salve's Regiment was officially incorporated into the line as a regiment of Marines, with De Salve promoted to Major General; Accara and Gousarie, who had helped capture over 600 runaway slaves, were acquitted and as a reward enlisted as free men into the regiment.

The Reign of Willem V

When Princess Anna died, the Duke of Brunswick-Wolfenbüttel assumed the role of regent to the young Prince of Orange, together with the prince's grandmother, Dowager-Princess Marie-Louise (until her death in 1765) and for one year with the prince's sister, Princess Carolina. Brunswick-Wolfenbüttel had been offered command of British and Prussian armies in the Seven Years War, but had declined, choosing to stay in the Republic. His influence on the matters of state and on the education of the young prince – who referred to him his 'second father' – was immense. Prince Willem said he valued advice, but, given his indecisiveness, and his tendency to lose himself in the smallest details, he had little interest in matters of state and signed whatever official document was laid in front of him, without bothering to read it first.

As a young boy, he had fallen of a horse; he lost two front teeth, which gave him a pout, and he had a limp. Although not a looker (he would later be described as 'an ugly little kraut'), he was quick-witted, had a great memory and a gentle character. In 1758, Colonel Douwe Sirtema van Grovestins of the *Guarde du Corps* and Equerry to the Stadtholder, who had raised him in his early years and was a confidant of Princess Anna (and, according to some, even more than that), was the centre of a scandal when it became known that he had acquired funds for 44 troopers on paper that he never recruited, and that he had bought copper lace instead of gold lace for the uniforms. The then 10-year old prince openly declared he 'only wanted to be around honest people', and Sirtema van Grovestins fell out of favour at court. It would be the beginning of the end of the influence of the Orangist Frisian nobility at court, and give Brunswick-Wolfenbüttel a stronger grip on government.

On 8 March 1766, his 18th birthday, Prince Willem assumed the position of Stadtholder. Given that the *Raadpensionaris* and several other members of the States of Holland and the States General did not see the young Stadtholder fit to be head of state and commander of the armed forces, Brunswick-Wolfenbüttel was appointed as guardian in the *Acte van Consulentschap* (Act of Consultation), a secret contract which stipulated that 1) the Duke would advise and assist the prince in military and state matters, 2) he would do so without bias towards states, provinces, or towns, but with the common interest in mind, 3) the Duke would permanently accompany the prince on all his travels, and 4) the Duke would not be held accountable or responsible by anyone, except by the prince. This made Brunswick-Wolfenbüttel *de facto* the head of state; and he need not worry that the prince would ever hold him accountable for anything. His influence grew even further when he arranged the prince to marry his 16-year old niece, princess Wilhelmina of Prussia, on 4 October 1767. The Republican factions had welcomed the period after the death of Princess Anna, who was said to have been a harsh and arrogant ruler, heavily influenced by the Frisian nobility. Brunswick-Wolfenbüttel had always been on good terms with the Republicans; at one point, they even wanted him to be proclaimed Stadtholder. However, it was now unacceptable to them that he continued to act as guardian of the prince, and thus have so much influence on the affairs of state. Even his niece Wilhelmina, who soon stepped in when her husband showed little interest and decisiveness in ruling the nation, began to resent 'the fat duke', as his opponents called him.

Meanwhile, Brunswick-Wolfenbüttel worked tirelessly on improving the army. In 1766, he had organised and professionalised the general staff, and regulated uniforms for general officers. The prince was to have a staff of seven uniformed adjutants. Also from that year on, uniforms and equipment became tighter, in the Prussian fashion, and likewise the drill. Like the Prussian army, the way regiments and companies were organised and equipped became the responsibility of the captain-general, who dictated the colonels and captains how to manage their regiments and companies. The 'Prussification' of the army also included that orders were to be obeyed strictly, and any familiarity between officers and men was to be condemned, let alone if a soldier showed disrespect to his superior. All these changes were of course met with resistance, and many doubted that the Prussian system would be suitable for the army of the Republic. The rash, blind obedience demanded was contrary to the system that had been developed in the 17th and 18th centuries, which had learned the officers and men to be cautious when handling their weapons; although the idea of strict discipline appealed to many, and was regarded as indeed very useful, the harsh Prussian discipline would never be popular, as can be read in a letter from Henry Peckham, dated 3August 1769, describing his visit to Den Briel:

> There are twelve companies of soldiers quartered in the town; the Dutch uniform is blue, faced with red [most likely that of the 2nd company of the 4th artillery battalion], which is not so brilliant in appearance as the English and French uniforms. We attended the parade and were treated with much civility by an officer of the corps who could speak English. The parade being finished, a grenadier was flogged for drunkenness; he received twenty strokes with the flat of a broadsword over his clothes; a punishment as trifling as with us the offence is common.

The punishment administered was certainly nothing like the brutal *spitzrutenlaufen* of the Prussian army. Besides the differences in military culture, it was unthinkable that the Republic would ever again organise an army of 100,000 men for an aggressive, offensive campaign, like it once had. A small army to fight a defensive war is what many officers perceived, but for now, would not dare to speak out.

Lady Elisabeth Percy, Duchess of Northumberland, who visited the Republic in 1771, gave vivid descriptions of the Duke, and of the army:

> [Friday] May the 17th. [...] As soon as I had dined I went to see the review of the Dutch Guards, commanded by Duke Louis. [...] The regiment is of two battallions, which are very numerous. The Duke marched and wheeled with them with great alacrity for a man of his bulk, which however, caused him to perspire so copiously, that he was not only wet through all his cloaths, but even his sash, and he was obliged, during his exercise, to change his wig eight times. He has a constitution robust to a degree. [...] The regiment was really composed of fine men, but I think they are slower than the English in their evolutions.
>
> Saturday, May the 18th. [...] In the afternoon I went to the review of the Swiss Guards, who are commanded by General Sandoz. The Prince always on these occasions walks along the line bare-headed, with his hat in his hand [...]. The Swiss guards performed much quicker and better than the Dutch did the day before.

Several days later, she witnessed the grand manoeuvres at the Waalsdorper Vlakte:

> Thursday, May the 23d. [...] We had a noble army to review. The Prince of Orange's guardes du corps, 256 effective men; Maesdams dragoons, 269; the Prince of Weilbourg's horse, 270; Dutch foot guards, commanded by Duke Louis, 1,400; Swiss ditto, commanded by General Sandoz, 1200; in all 3395 men. [...]
>
> Saturday, May the 25th. I was awaked by the drums a quarter before four, and as it was light, and my shutters are never shut, I sat up in my bed, and putting aside my curtain, saw Duke Louis, and his whole corps of 1400 men march by my window. At quarter before six, Algernon and I got a coach and four, and followed to the scene of action, which is a very spacious, extended plain covered with heath, flanked on one side by a little wood, and on the other by sand hills. The multitude of spectators which covered the latter had a very fine effect. I drove to a large tent pitched for the Princess and her company. The most extraordinary circumstance was, that though I knew there were 4000 soldiers there, yet there was not one to be seen; the two armies, one commanded by the Prince of Orange, and the other by

> General Maesdam, was entirely concealed, the one in the wood, the other behind the hill. They soon issued forth and attacked those in the wood. We had the exact representation of a compleat battle; and sometimes one had the advantage, and sometimes the other; we had retreats, rallying, skirmishing, &c. and at last one army entirely destroyed the other. The military people present assured us, that nothing could be represented more exactly; and that, excepting slaughter (I wish it ever was to be excepted) it was a real battle. The tent in which we were was a great curiosity; it belonged to King William, and had been presented to him by some town in Flanders; it is very large, and hung with a fine calico, on which was printed allegorical representations of his life and actions, with the portraits of himself and Queen Mary, Prince Eugene, Duke of Marlborough, and all the heroes of those times. [...]
>
> When the battle was over, every officer was invited to take part of those refreshments, and at the head of every regiment the Prince had ordered tables to be set, and every soldier had as much beer, bread and cheese as he chose. How often have I known our poor soldiers, on a hot day, marching to Wimbledon Common, going through their exercise at a review, and then broiling back to London, overcome with heat and fatigue, without having tasted a bit or sup; and how popular would an attention of this kind (the expence of which would be very trifling) make our King.

Unwillingly, she also was present when an assassination attempt was made at Brunswick-Wolfenbüttel on Monday 27 May, during a military parade:

> All thing went on extremely well till after one fire, every thing stopped short at once. As I was at a distance I could not guess for some time what was the meaning [...]; this was occasioned by balls being shot out of some of the pieces, two of which went through a pioneer's apron, and the skirt of another man's coat; and the third wounded Mr. Pickedezoeller, an officer [Lieutenant Colonel A.F.W. Pieck van Zoelen, captain of the 11th company, Dutch Guards], very dangerously in the groin, as he stood next Duke Louis, for whom the favour was undoubtedly designed, as he is amazingly hated by all the people. The fat man was horribly frightened, and the running footman cried out, the soldiers meant to assassinate their master; and that the coup was meant for him.

The next day, an issue was ordered that 'no officer or soldier should presume to mention, in any matter, the transaction on the plain yesterday, in order, as it is said, to prevent quarrels', which Lady Percy was bewildered about, for 'this is a free country!' She was convinced even more shots had been fired. However, no mention of the incident was made in the newspapers. In the end, it would not be through violence, but through a smear campaign, and the scandal that followed when the 'Act of Consultation' was made public, that Brunswick-Wolfenbüttel would be removed from office in 1784.

All that still lay ahead. The fourth quarter of the 18th century would be a time of turmoil, in which the Republic and the position of Stadtholder would come to an end. For now, the year 1772 saw the publications of the 'Regulations and General Orders for the Infantry Regiments of the State', the culmination of all the changes Brunswick-Wolfenbüttel had introduced. It was designed to improve uniformity in clothing and equipment. It ordered that service records be kept by the captains, in order to avoid conflicts regarding terms of service or fraud.

The year also saw the return of Major Fourgeoud, the veteran of Berbice, to the Americas as colonel of a newly raised regiment of marines, to fight in Suriname against runaway slaves and *Marron* tribes, led by the legendary leader Boni. One of the officers that volunteered was a Lieutenant John Gabriel Stedman of the 6th company, 2nd battalion of Stuart's Regiment of the Scots Brigade; his diary would be the basis of the book *Narrative of a five years' expedition against the revolted Negroes of Surinam*, which was published in 1796.

In 1772, Pieter Johan van As was no longer an officer. His first pay he had received on 9 September 1729, when he was but seven years old and a cadet in the Carabinier Regiment, serving in his fathers' company. His last pay he had received on 25 March 1771, as a lieutenant in the grenadier company of d'Envie's Regiment. He had had a horse shot from under him at Fontenoy; he had witnessed the siege of Bergen op Zoom; he had been captured at Fort Lillo and escorted into captivity. His pension after almost 40 years was an annual sum of 300 guilders, 'truly very meagre for such a long and dangerous service', as he wrote in his journal. Thanks to the Stadtholder, it was increased to 400 guilders. He died in the morning of 16 June 1801, six years after the Stadtholderate and the army in which he had served had ceased to exist.

4

The Artillery, Specialist Troops, and Staff

In 1576, Louis de Bloys was appointed Artillery General, holding the overall command of the artillery of the States army. He did not enjoy this title for long, since he was captured in May 1577, but was also suspected of collaboration with the enemy. His successor was appointed in August, but declined four days later. Number three was declared a rebel and a traitor in June 1578; number four quit the job in December 1579.

Despite this not-too-eventful start of this branch, the artillery became more professional and organised during the 17th century. The title of Artillery General changed to *Meester Generaal der Artillerie* (Artillery Master-General) in 1625; this commander, and the Lieutenant General (a rank created in 1577) were appointed from the infantry, whereby the Master-General of the Artillery simultaneously held the rank of Major General of the Infantry. By 1674, the artillery still had no permanent organisation, with matrosses and carpenters being recruited for the duration of the war; the captains of the ad hoc companies were appointed by the Stadtholder. War with France brought several flaws to light, which made the States General decide upon the creation of six permanent artillery companies. Colonel Johan de Bye van Albrandsweerd was appointed Colonel of the Artillery in 1677, with the same function as the Lieutenant General, and given the command of the newly created artillery regiment, in which the companies were organised. The companies, each of 188 men, were not numbered, but known by the name of their *inhaber*. Two companies were disbanded in 1678; but in 1698, four new companies were added.

The artillery had been part of the train, as were the sappers, miners, and pontoon troops. These specialists were organised into companies for the duration of a campaign, with their officers usually appointed from the infantry. In 1672 and 1677, these troops were organised into permanent companies. The 18th century saw the standardisation of materiel and armament, although for transport and labourers the companies still relied on civilians and carts that had to be mobilised.

Watercolour copy of a colourized print of the kettle drum cart, around 1700; from the *"Atlas [...] van het Artillerie-Materieel ten tijde van Prins Willem III, Koning van Engeland, 1691–1703"*. (Vinkhuijzen Collection)

The Artillery During the 18th Century

After the War of the Spanish Succession, with an immediate decrease of the army, the artillery also threatened to fall into decline. It was up to the officers to prevent that. In 1718, the captains were ordered to have their companies gathered for drill once every year, and from 1723 onwards the companies practiced with live rounds every other year, for which 600 lbs of gunpowder was acquired for each company. But the years of peace had taken their toll. After having assumed command of the artillery in 1735, Lieutenant General Van Glabbeeck toured the several garrisons to witness these exercise of the companies. His reports were not good: many officers, even the veterans from the last war, were inadequate and not suited for their task. Most were unable to construct emplacements and trenches, and none could make any explosives. He therefore ordered that, starting immediately in 1735, the artillery companies would gather every two years in Maastricht, Namur, Tournay, and Ypres, for 'grand exercises'; these consisted of the construction of a battery, a mortar emplacement, fascines, and 'everything that in times of war is related to the artillery'. He advocated the founding of an artillery school, but this never came to pass. Nevertheless, he took it upon him to improve the situation with dedication and hard work. Van Glabbeeck was not subtle in his actions, which led to confrontations with other officers, and even the Council of State. He was reprimanded for transferring officers in between companies; but he did manage that from 1743 onwards, within each company, 10 men would be rewarded for excellence, as an incentive.

With the augmentation of the army in 1747, four new companies were raised; all companies now consisted of a captain and his boy, a lieutenant and his boy, three fire workers, two artificers, four sous-lieutenants, 12 bombardiers, 88 gunners, 14 carpenters with two corporals, and 112 matrosses with eight corporals, 249 men in total. One more company was raised in 1748 and two more in 1749, making a total of 15 companies. The augmentations also led to the creation of the rank of Artillery Major General. The companies were organised into battalions, although this was an ad hoc

Model of a forge wagon, second half 18th century. (Rijksmuseum)

organisation, based on seniority of the company commanders. Only after 1751 was there a more permanent organisation of the artillery companies in three battalions of five companies each, with the strength of each company set by article XIV of the 1752 resolution as 125 men, viz. one captain, one captain-lieutenant, two artificers, three sous-lieutenants, nine bombardiers, 98 gunners, eight carpenters with two corporals, and one *schrijver*.

After the war, a new energetic Major General was appointed as commander of the artillery. Leopold Stephan Baron Von Creutznach (1702–1773) had been commander of the artillery of the Franconian *Reichskreiz* for 26 years before entering the States' service. After an inspection tour, he made a number of suggestions to enhance the effectiveness of the artillery, which the Stadtholder approved, and from which he received much support from Brunswick-Wolfenbüttel and the States General. First of all, Von Creutznach abolished the system of supplementing the artillery personnel with auxiliaries from other units or civilians, stating that the size of a company should be determined by the number of artillery pieces and the tasks required. New companies were therefore raised and the companies themselves increased. Second, he advocated standardisation and improvement of cannon and equipment. In 1750, he was appointed inspector of the cannon foundries, overseeing the casting of new barrels, where he standardised the design of the artillery pieces. Regular practice and constant experimenting led to the development of more effective ammunition. He also emphasised training the artillerymen in the use of the musket with which they were armed, but had grown to dislike. The artillery was now ordered to perform guard duties, alongside the infantry. Foundries, powder mills and magazines were reorganised and rebuilt, with the addition of an arms factory in Culemborg in 1759 to produce muskets. Throughout the third quarter of the 18th century, until his death in 1773, Von Creutznach worked tirelessly on improving the artillery, the excellent results of which were presented at the artillery camp in Breda in 1769, where five companies demonstrated the effectiveness of the cannon and mortars against a mock fortification. Those that succeeded him only had to continue upon the path he had laid out.

Dutch muskets from the 18th century; left: a Liège musket, around 1720–1740, which closely resembles the British Brown Bess muskets. In the middle, two muskets from around the same time, produced in the Republic, with typical brass furniture (after a watercolour by J. Hoynck van Papendrecht, from examples in the former Musée d'Artillerie). At right, the musket as produced from 1769 onwards in the Culemborg armouries (after an original in a private collection). (Author's drawing)

Field Artillery

The various calibres used in the artillery in the 16th century were standardised by Prince Maurice in 1590 to 48, 24, 12 and 6 lbs. The 48-pounders disappeared early in the 17th century; the 24-pounder guns were only used in sieges, since these were far too heavy to manoeuvre on the field (although the French used some during the Battle of Rocoux). Therefore, the largest pieces used in battle in the 18th century were the 12-pound cannon, slow firing, long range pieces with an effective range of 3,000 paces or 900–1,500 metres (maximum 2,300 metres), used against walled enemy positions and strongholds. If threatened by cavalry, rounds of *druiven* (lit. 'grapes', i.e. grapeshot), consisting of 24 ½-pound bullets, could be fired. The preferred piece was the 6-pounder cannon, with which a crew of eight men could fire two or three well aimed shots in a minute; if need be, this could be sped up to nine shots in a minute, though only for a short time, since the barrel would become very hot. For each 12- or 6-pounder gun, the ammunition carts transported 100 rounds of solid shot and 25 cases of grapeshot. This number was increased in 1747 and 1748.

The 3-pounder cannon, introduced in 1668, were used for infantry support at close range (150–300 metres). These were manned by a crew of five men, and could easily be transported with a pair of horses. The long version had a longer effective range, and was used to fire roundshot and canister, a tin cartridge filled with musket balls. The short version was used for *gezwindschieten* [rapid firing], a specialty of the Dutch artillery since its invention in 1689. For this, the crews used special ammunition, and they had trained to fire about 10 rounds in a minute. In 1746, a record was set during a demonstration for Marshals Batthyányi and Waldeck: a crew managed to fire 18 rounds in a minute – six more than their Hanoverian colleagues – and their commander, Lieutenant Martfeld, expected this could in the future be improved to 20 rounds a minute. On campaigns, there were 200 rounds for every piece. Finally, howitzers were used in the field

Model of grapeshot, second half 18th century. (Rijksmuseum)

Depiction of the artillery camp at Breda, 1769. (Rijksmuseum)

to throw explosive shells against entrenched or fortified infantry positions, with an effective range up to 2,000 metres. The specifications of the different pieces are listed below:

Calibre	Bore	Weight	Range	Length	Length (limbered)	No. of Horses
24-pounder	149.00 mm.	7.877 lbs	[none given]	25½ ft.	105 ft.	19
12-pounder	119.45 mm.	6.371 lbs	3,000 paces	24½ ft.	94½ ft.	15
6-pounder	96.00 mm.	4.327 lbs	3–5,000 paces	22½ ft.	82 ft.	11
Long 3-pounder	77.00 mm.	2.576 lbs	400 paces	18 ft.	48 ft.	7
Short 3-pounder	77.00 mm.	1.905 lbs	200 paces	12½ ft.	22 ft.	3
Howitzer	200.00 mm.	2.992 lbs	2,600 paces	16 ft.	46 ft.	7

Two innovations were introduced in 1746: the first was the use of cartridges, consisting of a powder charge and ball combined, which enabled more rapid firing. Every gun was distributed 40 of these (30 of round shot, 10 grapeshot) although their issue for the 12-pounders was discontinued after 1748). The second was the solid casting of barrels and then drilling the barrel axis; this was an improvement over the previous method of casting a barrel around a core which often led to imperfections.

The number of guns with the field army increased during the first half of the 18th century, because, as Adriaan van der Hoop explained, 'the way wars are fought changes over time, and these days, the barrage of fire is decisive in battles as well as sieges'. A comparison of the number of pieces, compared to the size of the armies, is given below:

	War of the Spanish Succession	War of the Austrian Succession	
Field army:	Around 100,000 troops	25,000 troops (1743)	50,000 troops (1746)
12-pounders:	8	8	6
6-pounders:	28–30	12	12
3-pounders:	24–26	30	50
Howitzers:	6	6	6

Emphasis shifted to lighter pieces, to make the artillery more mobile and give better support to the infantry, where each infantry battalion was accompanied by one 3-pounder gun; but against an enemy that had strengthened his position, as at Fontenoy, the 3- and 6-pounders had little effect.

Korps Ingenieurs

Engineers served the provincial states, designing, building and improving fortifications and defensive works. Unlike their colleagues who worked on the dykes and waterworks, they were regarded as military engineers. An *Inspecteur-generaal der fortificatiën* (Inspector-General of the Fortifications) was appointed in 1688, and all military engineers were united into one corps, called the *Dienst der Fortificatiën* (Fortification Branch). Inspector-General Menno Baron van Coehoorn, Vaubans' counterpart (and inventor of the small mobile mortar that bears his name), organised the engineers into three classes. He also created the rank of *directeur der approches* (Directors of the Siege Lines), engineers that commanded and directed siege works. These were organised in two classes in 1710. In 1713, an engineer was appointed to every fortress. If more engineers served in the same fortress, the *Eerstaanwezende Ingenieur* ('Engineer first present'; senior engineer) held overall command. These senior engineers were organised in 1714 into departments called *Eerstaanwezendschappen* led by a director.

The various directors and engineers held ranks in the infantry; the inspector-general was also a general in the infantry. In 1740, the name of the fortification branch changed to *Korps Ingenieurs* [Engineer Corps]; the ranks were as follows:

Ranks in 1740	Ranks in 1750
Directeur 1e klasse (Director 1st class)	Colonel-Director
Directeur 2e klasse (Director 2nd class)	Lieutenant Colonel-Director
Ingenieur 1e klasse (Engineer 1st class)	Major-Engineer
Ingenieur 2e klasse (Engineer 2nd class)	Captain-Engineer
Ingenieur 3e klasse (Engineer 3rd class)	Lieutenant-Engineer
Extra-ordinaris-ingenieur (Engineer extraordinary)	Remained unchanged.

Sappeurs, Mineurs, and Pontonniers

The artillery park brought pioneer equipment, which was distributed to detachments of infantry. The *timmerlieden* of each regiment, with additional detachments of an officer and 30 musketeers, were thus employed for clearing roads and removing obstacles. For the constructions of defensive works, the peasantry was pressed into service by the engineer corps, each man receiving a loaf of bread a day for his work. The work on siege lines and mines was considered too risky for civilians, and this was done by the sappers and miners. A company of sappers and miners had finally been established in 1689. In 1710, two *Detachementen Mineurs* (Miner Detachments) were added to the existing company; with the reorganisation of this company into a detachment in 1720, there were now three Miner Detachments, each of 32 men. A French company of Miners was captured by the end of 1747. Captain De Torcy Baron de Bréda, whose title had ties to the Orange-Nassau dynasty, offered his services and that of his company to the States General. He was ordered in February 1748 to expand the Miner Detachments to three companies of 150 men each, raise a fourth company, and organise these into a regiment of miners and sappers, of which he was appointed commander with the rank of colonel. Each company included 63 sappers and 63 miners. After the war, the companies were reduced in size, and according to article XV of the 1752 resolution set to one captain, one captain-lieutenant, two sous-lieutenants, two sergeants, two corporals, one drummer, one *schrijver* and 42 sappers and miners, a total of 52 men. In 1766, a colonel-commander was appointed, with De Torcy remaining as *inhaber* of the regiment. In 1769, the engineer officer Dumoulin became colonel-commander, and in 1776 *inhaber* of the regiment. Since he was also appointed Director-General of the Fortifications, he put his miners and sappers to work on improvements and repair on the various fortresses and defences.

A Pioneer or Miner, wearing a distinctive cap; detail of a print by Romeyn de Hooghe of the Royal Palace 't Loo, after 1700. (Rijksmuseum)

It was ordered in 1735 that when the artillery companies gathered for their joint exercises in the garrison towns of Maastricht, Namur, Tournay, and Ypres, the Sappers and Miners also had to show their abilities by constructing a gallery and a mine. Orders for these bi-annual aptitude tests were sent to the commanding officers of the three detachments and the garrison commanders; the exercise was observed by the Directors of the Engineer Corps during their annual visits in June, who sent their reports with their conclusions to the States General.

A company of *pontonniers* or *pontgasten* (pontoon troops) had been raised in 1672. These were responsible for storage and management of the material and equipment, kept in the storages at Dordrecht. The pontoons, known as *Blikken pontons* (tin pontoons), were invented by Willem Meester around 1670. The construction was a wooden frame, with an inner and outer work of tin plates soldered together into watertight separated compartments, giving the double-walled construction buoyancy. The rectangular pontoon measured 6.6 by 1.57 metres on the outside, 5.65 by 0.71 metres on the inside, and weighed 230 kg. It could carry up to 4,500 kg. This type had been introduced in the British and Spanish armies during the War of the Spanish Succession, and 16 of these pontoons were donated to the Austrian army in 1742. When war broke out, additional personnel were recruited among local sailors and boat

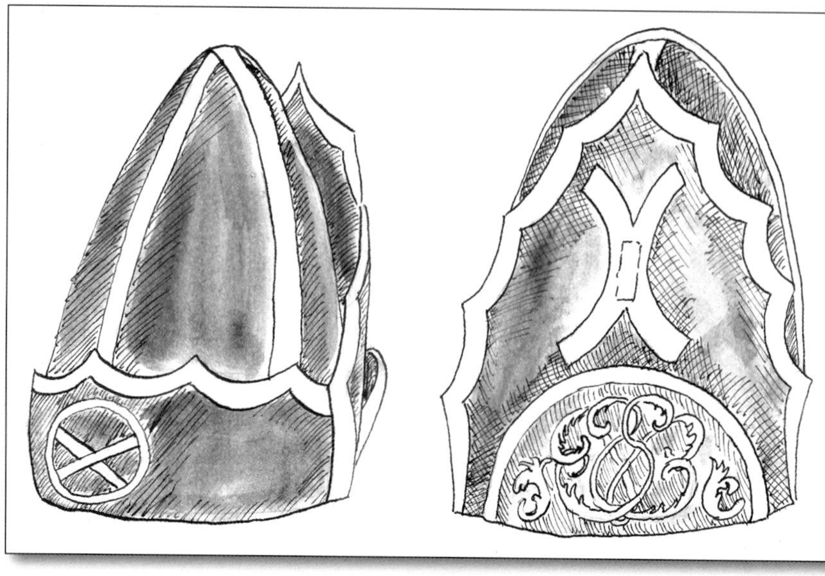

Back- and front view of a pioneer cap, from the collection at Castle Doorwerth, which was lost in 1944. The whole cap was made of red cloth, with white lace and white embroidered decorations. (Author's drawing)

masters. A pontoon train followed the army, while a pontoon fleet would sail up the rivers Rhine and Meuse. A train of 20 pontoons followed the corps that was sent to Germany in 1743, consisting of a lieutenant, a corporal, 31 *pontgasten,* a tin plate worker, and three carpenters, with 192 horses. The company took part in every campaign of the 18th century, and was continued after 1795.

Here follows an overview of the various units; where possible, the names of battles and sieges are added (see Part 1 for more information).

Regiment Artillerie, raised 1677

Inhaber from 1704 Master-General Van Goor (died 1705, succeeded by Colonel Ijssel), 1717 Lieutenant Colonel Verschuer, 1735 Lieutenant General Van Glabbeeck, 1748 Major General Von Creutznach.

Disbanded in 1795, when the foot artillery was reorganised into four separate battalions, which were combined with the Engineer Corps in 1807 into the *Koninklijke Korps der Artillerie en Genie* (Royal Corps of Artillery and Engineers).

According to the 1734 resolution, an artilleryman, like his colleagues in the infantry, would receive a kersey coat lined with baize, a ditto waistcoat and breeches, two hats, two pairs of stockings, a pair of gloves, two neck stocks and a shoulder cord. The artillery uniform throughout the 18th century was a dark blue coat lined red, with red cuffs and brass buttons; the colours of the waistcoat and breeches changed over the years. Bandoliers and *porte epée*s were of brown (buff) leather until 1753, when this became white.

Officers wore red smallclothes and stockings instead of blue until 1764. Rank designation as the infantry, viz. gold aiguillettes on the right shoulder, sash and sword knot, but no gorget. Coats were without embroidery or lace per regulations, although it seems officers had embroidered and laced coats for parade dress. Officers and NCOs were armed and equipped with fusils and belly boxes, until this was discontinued in 1774.

From 1705, the coat had Swedish cuffs; dark blue waistcoat, breeches and stockings. Officers: gold lace on the cuffs, hat decorated with gold lace and white plumes, red-white-blue sash around the waist.

1735: the coat now has red lapels; hat is decorated with gold lace and a black cockade. During the 1740s, a falling collar is added to the coat. Officers: orange sash worn over the right shoulder, hat with black cockade and gold lace, no plumes.

1753–1763: falling collar is discontinued and replaced with a small blue standing collar. Smallclothes become red for the NCOs and men.

1764: smallclothes blue, the officers follow suit. Shoulder strap of blue wool, no lace or piping. Officers wear the sash around the waist.

1769–1775: coat has straight red cuffs, falling collar, no lapels; shoulder flap blue with red piping. Smallclothes white. Officers and NCOs have scalloped gold lace on the hats. NCOs have a gold fringed epaulette on the right shoulder.

The Artillery Regiment had no colours, but instead a pair of kettledrums, mounted on a special cart that was drawn by two horses, the *heerpaukwagen*. The uniforms and equipment for the kettledrummer and driver were paid for by the Council of State. The cart was depicted on plate IV in the *Atlas of verzameling van teekeningen de inrichting voorstellende van het Artillerie-Materieel ten tijde van Prins Willem III, koning van Engeland, 1691–1702*, a work sadly lost, but copies of the plates survived. The kettledrummer was, also according to contemporary sources, a man of colour 'from Guinea', dressed in a semi-oriental uniform, consisting of a red coat lined blue, with blue large cuffs, red sleeved waistcoat and red breeches; the whole with gold buttons and elaborately decorated with gold lace. Blue stockings, blue and red turban with blue and red feathers. The driver wore a red coat lined red, with red cuffs and blue smallclothes and stockings, a black hat, all without decoration. Horse harness was blue, with red blankets.

Plate V of that same work showed a white drummer in a different uniform: blue coat lined red, with red cuffs and blue hanging 'false sleeves', gold buttons; the whole elaborately decorated with broad gold lace on the seams, 'false sleeves', around the cuffs (two rows) and the large pocket flaps (two rows, with ten buttons each). Red sleeved waistcoat with small gold buttons and decorated with gold lace; red breeches and stockings. Black hat with gold lace and blue ostrich feathers. The drummer appears to be wearing an orange belt or sash around the waist, over the unbuttoned coat.

In January 1747, the artillery kettledrummer Jan Welteling requested the Council of State to provide him with clothing:

> [L]ike the previous kettledrummers have received before, consisting of a red cloth coat, camisole and breeches, decorated with gold lace and blue velvet cuffs and lapels [*opslagen*] on the coat, and the coat of arms of the Generality embroidered on the back, with […] [a] *port epée,* a red cloth overcoat and hat with gold lace and plumes, doeskin gloves with gold fringe, red woollen [*sajet*] stockings and gilded sword.

A drawing by the engineer Dalhof, dated around 1754, shows the kettledrummer dressed in a red uniform, decorated with silver lace and red plume, while the driver is dressed in grey with red cuffs and lapels. The horses had scarlet blankets with gold fringe.

Dienst der Fortificatiën, raised 1688

Renamed *Korps Ingenieurs* in 1740; renamed *Korps der Genie* in 1806, but in 1807 organised with the artillery battalions into the *Koninklijke Korps der Artillerie en Genie.*

Inhaber from 1709 Le Vasseur des Roques, 1730 Hertell (until 1749), 1766 De la Rive, 1772 Stuten.

Since the military ranks were only created in 1740, it is safe to assume that uniforms were introduced in that year. All ranks wore a dark blue coat lined red, with red Swedish style cuffs and falling collar, gold buttons; red waistcoat and breeches. Directors had gold lace on the waistcoat, although that disappeared during the 1760s.

A new uniform was introduced in 1769, viz. light blue coat lined light blue, with black straight cuffs, lapels and falling collar, gold buttons. Light blue waistcoat and breeches. Gold lace around the collar, lapels and pocket flaps, two rows around the cuffs; and along the front and pocket flaps of the waistcoat. The engineers extraordinary, as junior officers, had no gold lace on the coat and waistcoat.

Compagnie Pontonniers, raised 1672.

Inhaber from 1693 Van Erp, 1722 Draak, 1746 Eggerink van Tiddinga.

The captains commanding the company were also officers in the Engineer Corps.

Not much is known about earlier uniforms, but these in all probability followed the example of the artillery. In 1769, the uniform consisted of dark blue coat lined white, with white straight cuffs and falling collar, pewter buttons. Dark blue waistcoat with white piping along the front and pocket flaps, dark blue breeches.

Compagnie Mineurs, raised 1672 as *Compagnie Mineurs* Nehr.

Disbanded in 1678, re-rased in 1689. Reorganised as *detachement* in 1720. Reorganised into a company in 1748 and incorporated as the 2nd Company into the *Regiment Sappeurs en Mineurs.*

Inhaber from 1706 Herman, 1720 Cuveler, 1725 Hougardy.

Battles: Ypres, Charleroi.

Detachement Mineurs Franken, raised 1710.

Reorganised into a company in 1748 and incorporated as the 4th Company into the *Regiment Sappeurs en Mineurs.* After 1795, this company became the 1st company of the newly raised *Corps Mineurs.*

Inhaber from 1710 Franken, 1731 De la Croix, 1763 de l'Age, 1769 Dumoulin.

Battles: Menin, Namur.

Detachement Mineurs Warroux, raised 1710.
Reorganised into a company in 1748 and incorporated as the 3rd Company into the *Regiment Sappeurs en Mineurs.*

Inhaber from 1710 Warroux, 1735 Barbonnes, 1738 Schreuder, 1741 Bourquin, 1748 De la Croix, 1770 Wagner.

Battles: Tournai, Maastricht.

Regiment Sappeurs en Mineurs, raised 1748.
Inhaber from 1748 Colonel de Torcy de Bréda, 1776 Major General Dumoulin.

Created from the three existing detachments and a newly raised 1st company. It was disbanded in 1795, and replaced by a newly raised *Corps Mineurs* (see *Detachement Mineurs Franken*).

Battles: Maastricht.

In all probability, the first uniforms were developed after the formation of the regiment, and it is likely it followed the example of the artillery, at first perhaps in grey, later in light blue or greyish blue. The first actual description comes from 1753, viz. light blue coat lined red, with red Swedish cuffs, red small standing collar, brass buttons. Red waistcoat and (presumably) red breeches.

1766: dark blue coat lined red, with red Swedish style cuffs and dark blue small standing collar, brass buttons. Dark blue waistcoat with red piping along the front and pocket flaps, dark blue waistcoat.

1769(?)–1775: dark blue coat lined dark blue, with black straight cuffs and black falling collar, dark blue shoulder strap with black piping, brass buttons. Dark blue waistcoat and breeches.

Generals and Staff

During the first half of the 18th century, the peacetime staff (besides the *Controleurs* of the fortifications and the artillery and commissaries of the army magazines and stores) was limited to three general officers, viz. a Quartermaster-General of the Army, a Quartermaster-General of the Cavalry and a Lieutenant General Quartermaster. At the beginning of a campaign, commanders, quartermasters, adjutants and other personnel would all have to be appointed. Stadtholder Willem V wanted a more permanent organisation, and so, a general staff was organised in 1752. The position of Quartermaster-General of the Infantry was created, and the office of Lieutenant General Wagon Master was made permanent. By 1760, the general staff consisted of the following:

- One *Generaal-kwartiermeester van de legers* (Quartermaster-General of the Armies)
- One *Generaal-kwartiermeester van de Infanterie* (Quartermaster-General of the Infantry)
- One *Generaal-kwartiermeester van de Cavalerie* (Quartermaster-general of the Cavalry)
- One *Luitenant-generaal kwartiermeester* (Lieutenant General Quartermaster)
- One *Kapitein der Pontons* (Pontoon Captain)
- One *Luitenant-generaal Wagenmeester* (Lieutenant General Wagon Master)

Portrait of Gerrit Sichterman (1688–1730), Quartermaster-general of the cavalry, *inhaber* of the Oranje Stad en Lande Regiment and commander of Grave, by Cornelis Troost, 1725. (Rijksmuseum)

Portrait of Lieutenant General Volbergen, commander of Bergen op Zoom, 1760. (Collection Museum Het Markiezenhof, Bergen op Zoom)

In 1766, there were two Lieutenant General Quartermasters, one for the infantry and one for the cavalry. To every general, an adjutant was appointed; the Stadtholder was to be assisted by a number of *Adjudanten van Zijne Doorluchtige Hoogheid* (Adjutants of His Serene Highness). The corps of *Guides* that was part of the train, was now added to the organisation.

The formation of a permanent general staff led to the development of uniforms and rank designations. General officers usually wore a uniform of their choosing, but, during the first half of the 18th century, dark blue was the colour of preference for the coat, with elaborate gold lace and floral embroidery. This led to the adoption of a uniform for generals in 1750, consisting of a dark blue coat lined red, with dark blue full cuffs, gold buttons, and elaborate gold lace and floral embroidered decoration; red waistcoat with gold lace, red breeches and red stockings; hat with gold lace, black cockade and black ostrich plumes. It is suggested that there was a form of rank distinction through the amount of gold lace and embroidery, but this is based on the comparison of portraits; there seems to have been no clear regulation at the time. In 1750, Willem IV ordered that the ranks for the general officers of the army and navy were to be more regulated, and to be linked together; this meant that rank distinctions for the general officers of the army and the navy were to be similar from now on. In 1766, it was stipulated that the general officers of the army and navy would wear the dark blue uniform with red waistcoat and breeches as prescribed for the army, but with rows of gold broad 'waved' lace; the navy officers had red cuffs instead of blue. Rank distinction was as follows:

Lieutenant General Jedze Edzard van Burmania, portrait by J.J. Heinsius, dated 1766. He commanded one of the regiments sent to Britain in 1745, and was captured at Rocoux the next year. Dressed in the generals' uniform, he holds a map of the battle. (Dekema State Jelsum)

Portrait of General Berend Lewe van Aduard, dated after 1772. The former commander of Tournai in 1747 is here shown in the full dress of a general officer, as stipulated in 1766. (Groninger Museum, on loan from J.T. Carp-Heijbroek, photo by John Stoel)

Army	Navy	Rank distinction
Major General	*Schout-bij-Nacht*	Single row of lace on the cuffs
Lieutenant General	*Vice-Admiraal*	Double row of lace on the cuffs
General of the Infantry, General of the Cavalry	*Luitenant-Admiraal*	Double row of lace on the cuffs, and a row along the front seams of the sleeves.

Adjudanten

Every general had an *adjudant* (adjutant). The Stadtholder had seven, organised into the Adjutants of His Serene Highness and divided into 1st, 2nd and 3rd Class; the whole was led by an *Adjudant-generaal*, Lieutenant General Rouse. When Rouse died in 1762, the position was vacant until the appointment of Major General Daniël Isaac Baron Cronström in 1766. He died two years later, his position taken over by Major General Van Tuijll van Serooskerken. There was one Adjutant 1st Class, two Adjutants 2nd Class and four Adjutants 3rd Class; no Adjutant 1st Class was appointed in 1763, instead there were now three Adjutants 2nd Class. In 1776, four Supernumerary Adjutants were added.

There is no information about the uniform for adjutants to the generals; this may have been a more modest version of the generals' uniform. The *Jassenboekje* only shows a sketch for the uniform in 1784. On the uniforms of the Adjutants of His Serene Highness, we have more information: a plate by La Fargue dated 1766 shows an Adjutant in full dress, viz. dark blue coat lined red, with red straight cuffs, red falling collar, gold flat buttons; bastion-

A print from a series on the household of Stadhouder Willem V, by Isaac de la Fargue van Nieuwland, dated 1766: an adjutant. (Rijksmuseum)

shaped lace loops of gold broad decorative lace, with large gold tassels, on the front (five evenly spaced pairs), cuffs (three each) and pocket flaps (three each), narrow gold decorative lace along the edge of the front, cuffs, collar and pocket flaps; turnbacks buttoned together. White waistcoat and breeches. Hat with gold lace, black cockade, gold button, white ostrich plumes. High cavalry boots, buff leather gloves, black stock. Orange sash around the waist, under the coat, the knot and tassels worn on the left side. Sword with silver grip. The *Jassenboekje* shows a formal dress and a field dress, dated 1768, which are almost similar: the formal dress is as described above, but there appear to be seven pairs of pointed lace loops of broad gold lace with tassels on the front, those on the cuffs and pocket flaps of narrow gold lace, with tassels; the field dress is the same, but all lace loops of narrow gold lace, and only those on the front (eight pairs) with tassels.

Corps Guides

At the start of a campaign, a number of officers and men from the cavalry regiments would be organised into an *ad hoc* unit of *Guides* (Scouts). Schlippenbach wrote about the formation of such a unit when the army marched to Germany in 1743:

> We all had a good laugh when our younger officers heard about the formation of a unit of over one hundred cavalrymen, either for reconnaissance or other tasks. The younger officers spoke to each other: "Dear God, what could it mean? Look, a detachment wandering off!"

In 1745, a permanent corps of *Guides* was formed, led by Captain Baron d'Eyschen of the infantry regiment d'Envie; he would continue to command this unit (whilst remaining owner of an infantry company) until his death in 1779. The unit consisted of one captain-lieutenant, one *wachtmeester* (NCO), 19 'ordinary' guides and five 'extraordinary' guides. It was part of the train, like the companies of Sappers and Miners and the Pontoon company; the captain-lieutenant reported to the Quartermaster-General. The unit inspected the roads along which the army would march; if any roads had to be cleared, members of the unit were to be present. The officers and men were therefore expected to know different languages, and be knowledgeable about geography. With the formation of the general staff in 1752, the corps became part of the staff organisation. It is likely that there was no uniform prescribed for the unit after its formation, the officers drafted from the various cavalry units still being dressed in the uniforms of their respective units. An illustration in the *Jassenboekje* suggest a uniform was introduced as late as 1784, consisting of a dark blue coat lined red, with red cuffs, red collar, dark blue lapels, and brass buttons, and white waistcoat and breeches.

5

The Cavalry and Dragoon Regiments During the 18th Century

As with the infantry, there were many cavalry regiments raised during wartime, but as soon as the hostilities were over, the number of regiments decreased rapidly. Holland had the largest establishment; in 1702, the provinces each provided for the following numbers of infantry battalions and cavalry regiments:

Holland: 19 battalions and 21 cavalry regiments (including guards and dragoons)
Friesland: 7 battalions and 2 cavalry regiments (*Guarde du Corps* and Life Guards)
Zeeland: 4 battalions and 3 cavalry regiments
Utrecht: 5 battalions and 1 cavalry regiment
Groningen: 3 battalions and 1 cavalry regiment
Gelderland: 3 battalions and 1 cavalry regiment
Overijssel: 2 battalions and 1 cavalry regiment
Drenthe: 1 battalion

After the War of the Spanish Succession, a number of cavalry regiments were disbanded immediately. In 1716, the Council of State ordered that when either the colonel-proprietor or the colonel-commander died, the regiment would be amalgamated with another regiment, thereby keeping the remaining regiments up to strength. This led to a steady decline in the number of regiments: there were 24 line regiments in 1713; 14 in 1726; nine in 1752; and six in 1763. After one more regiment was disbanded in 1771, the remaining five regiments would see action in the Revolutionary Wars. The line dragoons numbered five regiments at the end of the War of the Austrian Succession, but were reduced to three when the war was over, and two after 1752. Finally, in 1795 under the Batavian Republic, the guard units were all disbanded and the debris of the cavalry and dragoon regiments were reorganised into two regiments of heavy cavalry and one of dragoons.

A horse market; print by Jan van Huchtenburg, 1702. (Rijksmuseum)

Regimental and Company Organisation

The 'Incorporation Project' of 1752 changed much in regard of company and regimental strength for the cavalry and dragoons. Before that, every cavalry regiment had six to 10 companies, and more or less troops and staff per company. Although there should have been one *wachtmeester* in each company, a second *wachtmeester* had remained unofficially on the muster rolls since these had been abandoned in 1749, taking the place of a trooper; the guard companies also had a *picqeur* (horse master) and two trumpeters. The line regiments had kettledrummers, *picqeurs* and other personnel, which were not listed as such, but were funded nonetheless. It was decided that a company should from then on consist of one *ritmeester,* one lieutenant, one 2nd lieutenant or *cornet,* two *wachtmeesters,* one trumpeter, one *solliciteur*, three corporals and 36 troopers, a total of 46 men; the Guard cavalry would have both a 2nd lieutenant and a cornet, thereby having a total of 47 men. Each regimental staff would consist of a colonel, a major, an adjutant and a surgeon, to which were added a lieutenant colonel, a *picqeur*, and a kettledrummer.

The dragoon regiments were structured like the infantry regiments, and had one 'battalion' of ten companies each. However, in 1749, they were reduced by one company, the funds being used to pay off the regimental debts. With the 'Incorporation Project' of 1752, the regiments were organised like the cavalry regiments into four squadrons of two companies each. Like the cavalry, the dragoon companies were severely undermanned: the Guard Dragoons had 30 dragoons (including corporals) in each company, instead of 40, although each company did have two sergeants, two drummers, and a *picqeur.* In the 'ordinary' regiments, companies consisted of no more than 24 or 25 dragoons and corporals, two sergeants (of which one was unofficial, as had been the situation in the cavalry companies) and one drummer; in Von Ditfourth's Regiment, almost every company also had a *picqeur.* Every

Cavalry squadrons, formed up in three lines, at the Battle of Malplaquet. Detail of a print by Jan van Huchtenburg, 1727. (Rijksmuseum)

dragoon company would now consist of one captain, one lieutenant, one ensign, two sergeants or *wachtmeesters*, one drummer, one *solliciteur,* three corporals and 36 dragoons, making a total of 46 men. The regimental staff would remain the same, viz. a colonel, a lieutenant colonel, a major, an adjutant and a surgeon, to which were added a *picqeur* and a drum major.

Armament and Exercise

Apart from the Carabineers, all cavalry regiments were heavy cavalry regiments. These were the shock troops that rode on large horses in dense rows, charging into the enemy lines. The first cavalry charge, as we know it today, was in all likelihood performed by a detachment of 300 troopers, commanded by Colonel Johannes Sirtema van Grovestins on 28 June 1702. On the morning of that day, they met a French unit of about equal strength. The French fired a volley, as was the tactic of the period; but instead of returning fire, the Dutch charged them head-on and chased them off the field. This was to be the doctrine for the heavy cavalry in the 18th century, although the 1714 and 1732 regulations still required the troopers to fire their carbines first, then the right hand pistol, and finally the left hand pistol, before drawing the sword.

The cuirass had been discontinued during the Nine Years War, but was reintroduced in 1707, to give the trooper more protection from the pistols and carbines of the French. The regimental commanders were also instructed to give their men iron *calotten* or 'crosses' for under their hats, and leather camisoles. 10,000 cuirasses were distributed among the regiments, but these

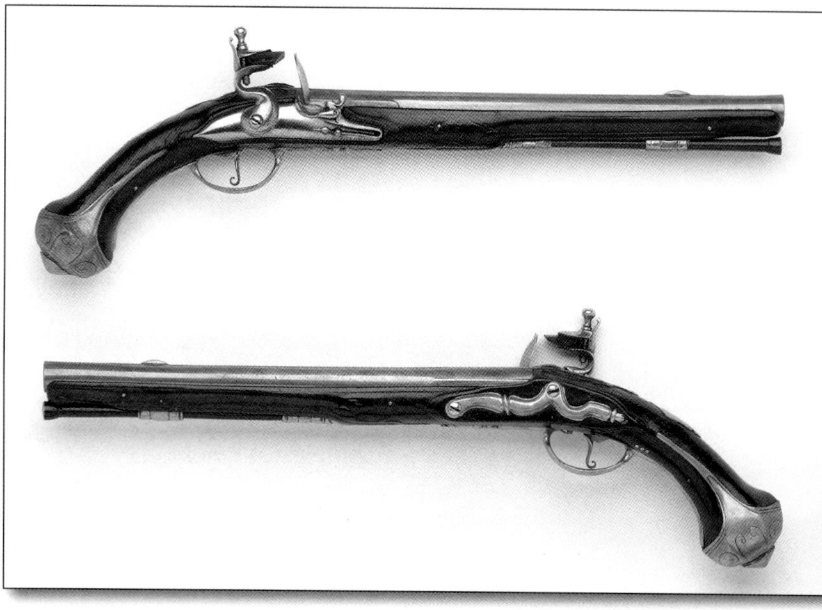

A set of cavalry pistols, made by La Haye, Maastricht, around 1730. (Rijksmuseum)

proved very unpopular: they were heavy and cumbersome, and if a trooper fell of his horse, he could get seriously injured. Many officers therefore had no cuirass in the field: for parades and reviews, they would show up with a cuirass on loan from a trooper or the depot. The officers' cuirasses were therefore required to have bright copper tacks, to distinguish them from the troopers' cuirasses. Nevertheless, many cuirasses were missing within two years after their distribution. Since many regiments claimed they had 'lost' their cuirasses in the Battles of Oudenaarde and Malplaquet, the Council of State decided to only reimburse the costs if the *ritmeesters* could prove they had been actually lost in battle, and that they had done their utmost to replace them. The remainder were evenly distributed among the regiments, to have at least the front ranks appearing in them. After the War of the Spanish Succession, the cuirass was again abandoned, as was the leather camisole. The broad carbine belt was expected to offer some protection to the chest.

The principal weapon for the cavalry was the *pallas,* a straight heavy cavalry sword, with an overall length of about three and a half *voet* (109.9 cm), the blade measuring about 35½ *Rijnlandsche Duim* (92.7 cm). Added to that was a carbine of four *voet* and four *duimen* (126.6 cm), and two pistols, all of a calibre of '18 to a pound'. Dragoons had longer carbines with bayonets of about one and a half foot (47.1 cm) long.

The heavy cavalry fought in three dense ranks, the troopers close to each other, so that the high topped riding boots of the trooper touched those of the man next to him. Dragoons, originally mobile infantry, and the Carabineers, fought on horseback like the heavy cavalry, but were also used for skirmishes and reconnaissance and could fight on foot if necessary. The regulations included an exercise for fighting as infantry for both cavalry and dragoons, (although the cavalry would not make much use of it). The squadrons would dismount to form a battalion of two ranks, the troopers shouldering their carbines, and the dragoons their muskets with fixed bayonets. When

Illustration by Mark Allen, see Colour Plate Commentaries for captions and further details.

Illustration by Mark Allen, see Colour Plate Commentaries for captions and further details.

Illustration by Mark Allen, see Colour Plate Commentaries for captions and further details.

The inspection of the Hesse-Homburg Regiment, 1742 by C. Troost. (Rijksmuseum.)

Illustration by Mark Allen, see Colour Plate Commentaries for captions and further details.

Illustration by Mark Allen, see Colour Plate Commentaries for captions and further details.

Illustration by Mark Allen, see Colour Plate Commentaries for captions and further details.

firing a volley, the front row would not kneel down, thus following the infantry exercise for the 2nd and 3rd ranks. The free companies of dragoons and hussars mimicked the Austrian light cavalry, in tactics, dress, as well as behaviour, and were used for raids against enemy supply lines or as a protective screen for the army. The curved sabre of the hussars was also called a *pallas* at first, the word denoting a cavalry sword in general. The *sabretache* used by the hussars appeared only for a brief time in the early 1770s with the *Oranje-Friesland* Life Guards, but was again soon discontinued.

The dragoon exercise, as noted in Dibbetz' *Groot Militair Woordenboek,* mentions that carbines and pistols should be used against attacks from 'the Turks or a similar enemy', i.e. irregular cavalry, while the 'ordinary' enemy should be attacked with the sword. When attacking an enemy, the third rank could split up to emerge on the flanks and surround the enemy, depending on the situation. When the enemy was broken, it was important not to go after them with the entire squadron, but to send out small detachments, in case of an enemy counterattack. When forced to retreat, the squadrons would break up in sections, which would alternately move backwards, face front and keep the enemy at bay with the carbines whilst the next sections would move backwards and face front behind the first. Schlippenbach wrote how he covered the retreat of the infantry at Fontenoy this way.

The ideal recruit for the cavalry was not a giant of a man, but rather a robust young man between 20 and 30 years old, with a minimum height of 5 feet 6 inches, though not exceeding 5 feet 10 inches (roughly between 1.72 and 1.83 metres). Given the small size of the cavalry arm, there were enough recruits to find among the peasantry within the Republic, although being able to ride a horse was not a requirement. Only after the horse was well trained, and the recruit had learnt to ride a horse properly, was the recruit taught the cavalry exercise. The cavalry could not exercise as frequently as the infantry; therefore, the season for exercises was in March, April and May, until the horses were sent to summer grazing from 15 May. If the weather permitted it, the regiments practiced the manoeuvres on horseback twice a week in winter, while in summer, this was done every two weeks. This enabled the commanding officers to see if men and horses were still fit for duty.

When the dragoon regiments were again mounted in 1726, all captains received funds to buy sufficient horses. Schlippenbach wrote how every *ritmeester* in his regiment had their companies up to strength in a short time, except Van Nes, the troublemaker mentioned earlier. He had severely neglected his duties and spent the funds on liquor; the horses he did manage to get were either unfit or too old, most being old cart horses. After he failed to replace them, Schlippenbach had the horses inspected by the garrison commander, who wrote a report to the Council of State. They sent a commission to inspect the horses themselves. Thirty-seven horses were rejected, and Schlippenbach was given the task to bring the company up to strength. Within a year, he had replaced the 37 horses with sufficient mounts. Despite his mismanagement of affairs, of which Schlippenbach wrote extensively in his memoirs, Van Nes was never discharged and would be promoted to major in 1737 and lieutenant colonel in 1740. When the regiment was mounted again, they needed to exercise, which the officers seemingly resented: Major Jekermans had no knowledge of the exercise, so that Schlippenbach had to exercise the regiment himself, and the *ritmeesters* could only be persuaded to do so after complaints to the Council of State or court appearances for neglect of duty.

Uniforms and Equipment

Every two years. a cavalryman received a coat and waistcoat, both of broadcloth and lined with baize; leather camisoles are specifically mentioned in 1734 as being discontinued. Also a pair of breeches, a hat with fine gold or silver lace, a pair of gloves, two linen stocks or one silk stock, and a 'field sign' on the shoulder and on the sword, these being cords and straps. Every six years, each man was also given a cloak, housing and holster covers. In the Guard cavalry, every man received a hat with fine silver lace, a pair of gloves and two stocks every year, and every three years a broadcloth coat and waistcoat, both lined with *saay* (a finer wool), and a lace strap on his sword. Besides a cloak, housing and holster covers, every guardsman would receive a laced broadcloth carbine belt cover every six years. The dragoons received every three years a broadcloth coat and a kersey waistcoat, both lined with baize; a pair of breeches, a hat laced with either false silver or other, a pair of stockings and three stocks. Also every six years a cloak, housing and holster covers.

As with the infantry, the regulations stressed that the officers were forbidden to wear any gold or silver embroidery on the coats and waistcoats. The resolution of 11 March 1740 stated that this was punishable 'for the commanding officers by deduction of a half year's pay, for subalterns by deduction of a month's' pay.' Nevertheless, the use of gold and silver on uniforms, even those of the troopers and dragoons, was quite common, and certainly not limited to the Guard regiments. The portrait of Ludolf Bakhuyzen II in the uniform of a dragoon of De Berg Trips' Regiment shows buttonholes worked with silver thread and silver lace on the waistcoat, while the painting of the Hesse-Homburg Regiment shows the carbine belts of the troopers with silver lace trim. Schlippenbach recalls how his

Watercolours of cavalrymen, around 1730. (Vinkhuijzen Collection)

regiment received new uniforms in 1731, which had been ordered in the previous year. The order included an amount of silver thread for buttonholes and epaulettes. When the regiment was presented in the new uniforms, he noticed how Captains Van Nes and Vrijenes had the buttonholes worked with blue worsted wool lace:

> I asked them what the reason was for this anomaly. They said it was forbidden according to the regulations to wear uniforms which had been worked with gold and silver, and that they acted accordingly. I then ordered them to have their uniforms worked with white worsted lace and white wool epaulettes, just like the dragoons, because I wanted a regiment dressed in uniform, not in fancy dress costumes.

As can be expected, both officers were embarrassed, and thus agreed to the silver decorations. Oebschelwitz, in his *Militair Handboek voor de Cavallery* (Military Handbook for the Cavalry) in 1761, wrote how all this gold and silver could not be preserved properly when on campaign. He warned about light troops, who would only fight for plunder, and would risk life and limb to obtain just a hat with a gold or silver lace edge. Furthermore, he warned, that although some gold or silver lace and cords, as well as non-functioning lapels and livery cords, may seem like a small expense, but for an army of about 100,000 men this would in the end cost a fortune, and the amount of money wasted in this manner could be used much better. Even reusing the buttons of the old uniforms for the new would save thousands of guilders, not only for the common soldier, but also for the captain. After 1766, the hats no longer had lace, but a white feather plume was added.

The sword was carried on a waist belt, and the carbine on a broad carbine belt over the left shoulder. Dragoons would often have a small cartridge box, worn on a narrow belt over the right shoulder. Cavalry troopers are never

Studies of cavalrymen by Cornelis Troost, dated 1740. The hats are too small, but the drawings show details such as the buckles of the breeches and the stock. (Rijksmuseum)

shown with these on prints, despite their armament with a carbine, until the 1780s; It is suggested in the 1754 regulations that they wore a belly box.

Musicians and Standards

Officers tended to spare funds to have elaborately dressed musicians. Usually, every *ritmeester* would buy musicians' uniforms for the trumpeter or drummer of his company, and – if the regiment had a band –for the oboist; the colonel would pay for the uniform and instrument of the kettledrummer, a practice that was confirmed after 1752 when every regiment officially had a kettledrummer. These musicians would often have distinguishable uniforms, either in reversed colours, or in the livery colours of the *inhaber.* A common distinction were the *banderollen* or *trompettervleugels* (trumpetters' wings), long strips of cloth with lace decoration that hang from the back of the coat, which had evolved from false sleeves. Sometimes 'swallows' nests' were worn on the shoulder, usually in combination with the *banderollen*. The use of livery lace, or livery cords, in the heraldic colours of the *inhaber,* became popular during the War of the Austrian Succession; they are mentioned in a receipt for Hop's Regiment in 1744, although a receipt for the Rechteren-Zeeland Regiment suggest they were in use before 1741. The trumpets themselves are often depicted with cords and tassels instead of banners, as was usual in other armies. The kettledrums were decorated with elaborately embroidered covers, decorated with lace and tassels.

Information on standards of the cavalry and dragoons is scarce. The Regiment *Guarde du Corps* of Zeeland, later known as the Regiment Nassau la Lecq, carried a blue standard around 1700, while during the 1740s the *Guarde du Corps* on the Friesland establishment carried a carmine standard, according to a primitive watercolour of that time. The *Triomphes*-manuscripts, which portray the Allied flags, banners and standards captured by the French armies of Louis XIV and XV, show a number of standards, most in white with gold fringe; the cavalry standards were square, while those of the dragoons appear to be cut in a wedged *guidon* style. The standards depicted either as a centre device the coat of arms of the province or that of the *inhaber,* often with above or below a scroll with a motto, embroidered or painted on brocaded silk damask or plain silk. They were mounted on a lance, modelled after a medieval jousting lance.

All troopers and dragoons were expected to wear heavy blackened moustaches, those being regarded as a sign of bravery. It was forbidden to have these shaved off when on leave. Those too young and not sporting a full moustache yet could have one painted on, if necessary. The hair was worn according to the fashion of the day, which during the 1740s and 1750s meant it was tied up in a queue in a black ribbon, with *cadenettes* over the ears. These curls had to cover the ears, as this was considered to prevent the soldier catching a cold. The first real regulations on how to wear the hair in a braid is Article XI 'On Cleanliness', of the 1768 'Regulations for the *Guardes du Corps* Squadron', a reflection of the 'Prussification' of the army, which seem a confirmation of what was already military fashion:

Details of plate 13 from the series on the funeral procession of Stadholder Willem IV, by Jan Punt, 1753: officers of several cavalry regiments, in particular one of the States Hussars and of the regiment Schultz van Hagen (with embroidered decoration around the buttons holes). (Rijksmuseum)

> The *Guardes du Corps* must always wear their Dress hat, Coat and Waistcoat, and never appear otherwise in the Street; the Hair always dressed and with a Queue, when on duty or not, which hangs from the crown, from which a ribbon is worn at a hand's width.'

The hat was worn slightly tilted, the front point downward over the left eye, as this added to the *bon air* of the rider. Oebschelwitz in his Military Handbook wrote that the hats should have a leather strap or strong ribbon, so as to tie under the chin, to prevent the hat from falling off when worn in battle (although so far, no print or painting is found showing these straps).

The following chapters show a general overview of the cavalry regiments; although not so distinguished in contemporary sources (which only mention cavalry and dragoons), for the sake of clarity, the units are divided into guard cavalry, line cavalry, dragoons, and light cavalry. Needless to say this overview displays only the regiments active from 1713 until 1772. The name of the regiment is that of the *inhaber* in 1713, unless otherwise specified.

6

Guard and Life Guard Cavalry

During the 17th century, a number of guard units were raised, though after the reign of Willem III, three guard units remained: the 'Red Guards' (*Guarde du Corps*), the 'Blue Guards' (Horse Guards), and the Guard Dragoons. The *Guarde du Corps* began as a regiment on the Friesland establishment, but developed into a ceremonial company, which performed guard duties on foot around the residences of the Stadtholder, and accompanied him on horseback on travels. Also on the Friesland establishment was the *Oranje-Friesland* Life Guard Regiment, of which Willem IV was *inhaber*. As with the guard infantry regiments, the guard cavalry regiments were brigaded with the line cavalry during campaigns.

Guarde du Corps, raised 1685 (Friesland establishment).
The regiment consisted during the first half of the 18th century of two companies, organised into one squadron. The squadron was commanded by a *ritmeester* at first, until in 1697, *Ritmeester-commandant* Hilcken van Lorch was given the rank of colonel. After the War of the Spanish Succession, the *Guarde du Corps* was reduced to one company, which was dismounted for a brief time in the 1720s, until the augmentation of the army in 1726. In 1740, the company consisted of a colonel-commander, one major, two *ritmeesters*, one captain-lieutenant, four lieutenants and 86 troopers (all NCOs) with 94 horses. In 1744, there were again two companies, organised into one squadron. The regiment seems to have been disbanded in 1759, since it is not mentioned in the officers' registers in those years.

In 1766, a new *Guarde du Corps* was raised on the Holland establishment, consisting of one mounted company, now only performing ceremonial and guard duties. Ranks were as follows:

Rank	Equivalent	Held by
One Captain (Commander)	–	Stadtholder Prince Willem V
One *Ritmeester-commandant*	Colonel	Field Marshal Duke of Brunswick-Wolfenbüttel
One 1st Lieutenant	–	Major General Harinxma thoe Slooten
One 2nd Lieutenant	–	Colonel Van Wulknitz
One *Cornet*	–	Colonel Van Stöcken

One *Guidon* (standard bearer)	–	Major Raeber
Four *Exemts*	Senior captain	
Four Brigadiers	Senior Lieutenant	
One Adjutant	Lieutenant	

Added were a staff of one *auditeur* (judge-advocate), a surgeon and a *picqueur*. In 1769, some changes had been made in the command structure and the rank designation:

Rank	**Equivalent**	**Held by**
One Captain (Commander)	–	Stadtholder Prince Willem V
One *Ritmeester-commandant*	Colonel	Field Marshal Duke of Brunswick-Wolfenbüttel
One 1st Lieutenant	–	Major General Harinxma thoe Slooten
One 2nd Lieutenant	–	Colonel Van Wulknitz
One *Cornet*	–	Colonel Van Stöcken
One *Guidon*	–	Major Raeber
Four *Exemts*	Major	
Four Brigadiers	Captain	
One Adjutant	Lieutenant	
One Quartermaster	Lieutenant	
Four Sous-Brigadiers	*Cornet*	
Four Supernumeraries	–	

Inhaber from 1711 Van Hammerstein (major, from 1730 colonel), 1741 Sirtema van Grovestins (until his death in 1759), 1766 Duke of Brunswick-Wolfenbüttel.

In 1795, the squadron was disbanded.

At the beginning of the 18th century, the unit is referred to as the 'Red Guards', since the unit was dressed in red coats lined blue, with blue full cuffs, blue waistcoat and breeches, gold buttons; hat decorated with ostrich feathers; blue housing and holster covers. Romeijn de Hooghe shows troopers wearing a sort of cassock worn over the uniform, with a crowned 'W' on the sleeves. Trumpeters wear the same, but with small 'swallow's nests' and *banderollen*, heavily decorated with gold lace.

Officers' coats have red lining and cuffs, gold lace and buttons, red smallclothes; housing blue with gold lace.

During the first half of the 18th century, the members of the *Guarde du Corps* appear to have had two uniforms: a formal or parade dress, and a field dress. The former can be seen in several portraits: the portrait of Leonard Hoefft, dated 1730, shows a light blue coat lined ditto, with ditto full cuffs, gold buttons; gold floral embroidered decorative loops on buttons and buttonholes along the front (10 evenly spaced), on the cuffs (three) and pocket flaps (three). Light buff coloured waistcoat with gold embroidery along the edges. Portraits of among others Colonel Sirtema van Grovestins (1747) and Coenraad van Heemskerk show the uniform as described above, but with minor differences in embroidery and lace decorations. Portrait of Cornet Jan Diederik Pauw (1751) shows the waistcoat with broad gold lace along the edges. Portrait of Cornet Raeber (1753) shows buttonholes

Troopers and standard bearer of the Horse Guards, sketch in pencil and ink by La Fargue, 1770. (Collection Municipal Archives, The Hague)

Portrait of Coenraad, Holy Roman *Reichsgraf* van Heemskerk, 1750. (Rijksmuseum)

Portrait of Jacob van Kretschmar, later commander of the Dutch Guards, around 1750. The coat has lavish gold floral embroidery. The collar comes from under the cuirass and is not part of the coat. (Private collection, with kind permission by Mr C. van Kretschmar)

Portrait of Christiaan Albrecht van Rechteren, in the dark blue field uniform, dated 1740. (Stichting Collectie Van Rechteren-Limpurg, with kind permission by Mr N. Count Van Rechteren)

Two prints from a series on the household of Stadhouder Willem V, by Isaac de la Fargue van Nieuwland, dated 1766: colonel and trooper. (Rijksmuseum)

Playing card, depicting a Guarde du Corps, around 1750. (Rijksmuseum)

Stadtholder Willem V in the uniform of the Guarde du Corps; portrait by J.G. Ziesenis, 1770. (Rijksmuseum)

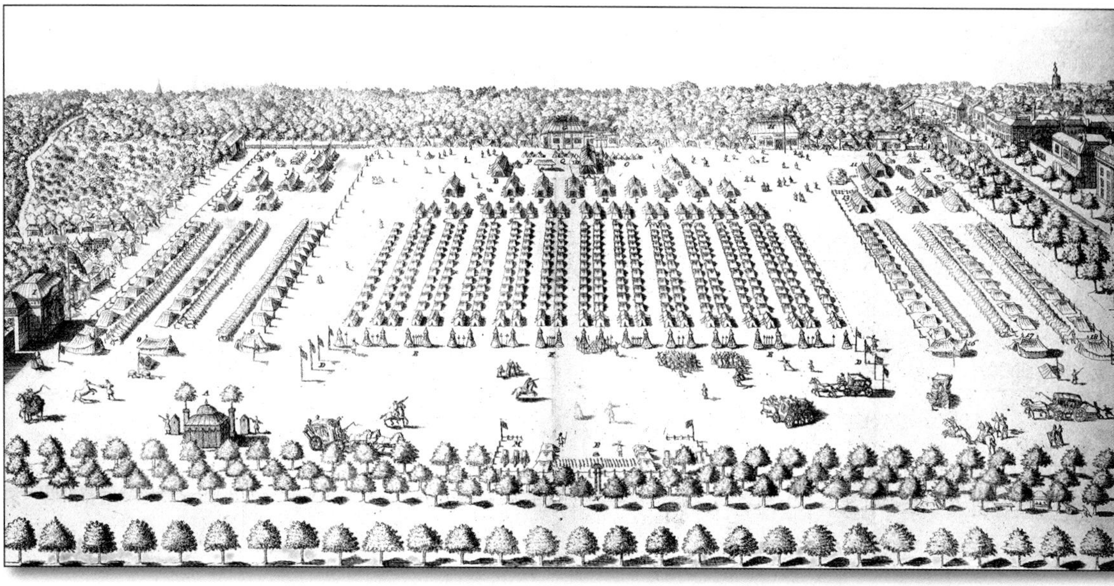

The camp of the Dutch Guards and Horse Guards at the Maliebaan in The Hague on May 29 1742. Print after Daniel Marot. (Rijksmuseum)

Sketches of the cavalry camp at the Malieveld in 1742 by Cornelis Pronk. (Rijksmuseum)

Details of plate 1 and 2 from the series on the funeral procession of Stadholder Willem IV, by Jan Punt, 1753: kettle drummer, trumpeters, colonel-commander and officers of the Horse Guards. (Rijksmuseum)

Detail from plate 3 from the series on the funeral procession of Stadholder Willem IV, by Jan Punt, 1753: Horse Guards, with the cavalry standard lowered. Notice detail of the embroidery on the housing and holster covers. (Rijksmuseum)

Contemporary drawing of a Horse Guards trooper with (presumably) a camp colour, 1763–1765. (Private collection, thanks to Mr P. Imthorn)

Detail of plate 4 from the series on the funeral procession of Stadholder Willem IV, by Jan Punt, 1753: troopers and NCO's of the Horse Guards. (Rijksmuseum)

Review of the Horse Guards at the Malieveld in The Hague by Prince Willem V, print by La Fargue. (Rijksmuseum)

P.C. la Fargue, del.

Horse Guards trumpeter, by La Fargue, 1770. Note *banderollen*, swallow's nests and cords and tassels on the trumpet. (Collection Municipal Archives, The Hague)

Black kettle drummer, presumably of the Horse Guards, drawing in pencil and ink by La Fargue, 1770. (Collection Municipal Archives, The Hague)

worked with gold thread, with gold floral embroidery around the edges. This uniform appears to have been replaced after 1753 by a dark blue uniform, similar to the field uniform, but with elaborate gold embroidered loops and gold aiguillettes; it is discontinued after 1766.

The field uniform can be seen in a portrait of Christiaan Albrecht Count Van Rechteren, dated about 1725–1730: dark blue coat with ditto lining and narrow round cuffs, gold buttons; button holes worked with gold thread and a small gold tassel (there are four on each cuff in this particular portrait). Yellow/buff waistcoat without decoration except gold thread on button holes. Orange sash around the waist under the coat. Others sources suggest gold lace loops for officers.

1750: troopers' uniform consists of a dark blue coat lined poppy red, with poppy red full cuffs, small dark blue standing collar, gold buttons and gold bastion-shaped lace loops on the front, cuffs and pocket flaps; front, cuffs and pocket flaps edged with gold lace. Yellow/buff waistcoat with gold lace edge and bastion shaped lace loops; yellow/buff breeches. Hat with gold lace, gold lace loop and black cockade. Housing red. Broad carbine belt and waistbelt, in poppy red with broad gold lace trim. Yellow/buff leather gloves.

1753: lace loops become straight (nine pairs on the front, three on the cuffs).

1766: a poppy red falling collar is added. Lace loops become 'cloverleaf-shaped' with tassels, as can be seen in the prints by La Fargue. On the left shoulder a gold lace epaulette with gold fringe. Hat with scalloped gold lace edge, narrow gold lace loop and black cockade, mounted by a white plume. Broad carbine belt poppy red with broad gold lace trim; buff leather waistbelt. For dismounted guard duty, a buff leather belly box with gilded emblem of a cypher, surrounded by the Order of the Garter and a crown, is worn. *Sous-Brigadiers* are dressed similarly, but with a gold aiguillette on the right shoulder instead of the epaulette, a white plume with black top on the hat, and an orange sash around the waist, under the coat. The *Ritmeester-commandant* has broad decorative lace along the edges of the coat and waistcoat, along the pocket flaps, and two rows along the cuffs.

1772: fringe on the gold lace epaulette disappears, gold aiguillette is added on the right shoulder.

Garde te Paard (Horse Guards), raised 1672 (Holland establishment). *Inhaber* from 1711 van Hompesch, 1733 van der Duyn, 1733 van Lynden, 1734 van Bentheim, 1748 van Hompesch, 1765 van Nassau-Weilburg.

The regiment consisted of two squadrons, but was expanded to three squadrons during the War of the Austrian Succession. The regiment was disbanded in 1795.

Battles: Germany, Rocoux, Lauffeld.

Known as the 'Blue Guards' at the beginning of the 18th century, the regiment wore blue coats lined red, with red full cuffs, white pointed lace loops and edge, silver buttons. Red waistcoat and breeches. Hat with white lace. A cassock, as mentioned with the *Guarde du Corps*, was also worn by the Horse Guards. Trumpeters as the troopers, but with gold lace decoration, wings and *banderollen* decorated with gold lace. Housing red with white lace.

Officers had silver lace decorations. The regiment wore blue and red uniforms with white lace throughout the 18th century; the housing and holster covers were red, with embroidered emblems of an armoured arm holding a sword, emerging from a cloud (in natural colours) on a red shield, below a scroll with the motto 'PRO PATRIA'; those of officers and NCOs red with two rows of silver lace, that of the colonel commander with lace and fringe.

1753: coat with full cuffs and lapels, dark blue cuff flaps and small standing collar, red shoulder strap (left), straight lace loops, silver buttons (seven evenly spaced on the lapels). Yellow waistcoat and breeches. NCOs have silver lace along the edges of the lapels, cuffs and pocket flaps; no lace loops on the lapels, only for the buttons under the lapels; they wear an orange sash around the waist (the bow apparently on the left side), officers ditto over the left shoulder. On the prints of the funeral procession of Willem IV, the housing and holster covers are blue with embroidered emblems for the troopers, though those of the NCOs and officers are red; this is in all likelihood a mistake by the colourist. Trumpeters and kettledrummer wear red coats lined blue, with red full cuffs, blue 'swallows' nests' and *banderollen*, gold buttons; blue waistcoat, yellow breeches. The whole heavily edged and decorated with gold lace. Hat with gold lace and black cockade; housing and holster covers red with two rows of gold lace.

1755–1762: lace only along the edges of the cuffs, cuff flaps and lapels. Around 1760, the cuffs change to the Swedish style.

1763: uniform is largely similar to that of the *Guarde du Corps*, viz. coat without lapels, and a red falling collar with white lace edge. Ten pairs of straight lace loops on the front (evenly spaced).

1766–1774: as the *Guarde du Corps*, but all lace white (also on the collar); white epaulette on the left shoulder, dark blue shoulder strap on the right. Musicians as the troops, with small swallow's nests and *banderollen* added, decorated with livery lace. Kettledrum covers show the coat of arms of the Stadtholder, surrounded by elaborate decorative embroidery.

Garde Dragonders (Guard Dragoons), raised 1672 as the Duke of Courland's' Regiment of Dragoons (Holland establishment).

The regiment was elevated to guard status in 1676 when Prince Willem III became *inhaber*. *Inhaber* from 1702 Willem Prince of Hesse-Cassel, 1747 Van der Duyn van Maasdam.

The regiment was disbanded in 1795.

Battles: Germany, Fontenoy, Rocoux, Lauffeld.

The Guard Dragoons wore uniforms like the other dragoon regiments, as can be seen in the painting by Morier of a dragoon on horseback, dated about 1748–1750. It is presumed to be of Trips' Regiment, but the coat has aiguillettes and lapels; the housing and holster caps have broad chequered lace and a narrow chequered lace edge and 'diamond' decoration. This is similar to the uniforms worn by the Guard Dragoons in the print of the funeral procession of Willem IV, dated 1752. It is therefore safe to assume the painting by Morier shows a guard dragoon. Other sources show white straight lace loops on the lapels (seven pairs, evenly spaced), plus three under the lapel, and one on the red shoulder strap. In 1752, the cuff is straight with

Plate 1 from the series on the funeral procession of Stadholder Willem IV, by Jan Punt, 1753: Guard Dragoons, on the entrance on the way to Delft. (Rijksmuseum)

a dark blue cuff flap with three lace loops. This changes to Swedish style cuffs with three lace loops around 1755–1759.

1760–1772: lapels are discontinued, cuffs become straight, a red falling collar is added. Ten pairs of straight white lace loops on the front. The fur cap with red bag and white lace and tassel is most likely introduced around the same time as the fur caps for the grenadiers of the Dutch Foot Guards, since they appear in no prints and paintings until the 1760s. In 1763, the aiguillette is replaced by a white fringed epaulette. The cuff style changes in 1772, closing vertically with four buttons (two on the cuff, two above), whilst the left shoulder strap is now of white lace. Officers have a single silver epaulette on the right shoulder, silver lace loops, silver lace on the bandoliers, ditto plus silver tassel on the bag of the fur cap. Several depictions of the Guard Dragoons on horseback show housing and holster covers with two rows of lace.

Dismounted cavalry, detail of a drawing of the mock battle at the Waalsdorper Vlakte, by La Fargue, 1771. On the left a guard dragoon. (Collection Municipal Archives, The Hague)

Regiment Oranje-Friesland, raised 1665 as Regiment *Nassau-Friesland* (Friesland establishment).

Renamed *Oranje-Friesland* in 1702. Also known as *Oranje Lijfregiment* or *Lijfregiment van Zijne Hoogheid* (His Highness' Life Guard regiment).

Inhaber from 1711 Willem IV of Orange-Nassau, 1751 Willem V of Orange-Nassau.

In 1795, the regiment lost its life guard status and became the *2e Regiment Zware Cavalerie*.

Battles: Rocoux, Lauffeld.

Uniform in the 1740s: grey coat lined red, with red full cuffs, brass buttons. Buff waistcoat and breeches. Red housing and holster covers. A watercolour by Troost in the British Museum shows (presumably) an officer in this uniform; the red housing is edged with broad gold lace.

1753: white coat lined red, with red full cuffs, lapels and small standing collar, brass buttons. Yellow/buff waistcoat and breeches.

1759: white coat lined dark blue, with dark blue full cuffs and lapels, white small standing collar, white shoulder strap with dark blue piping, brass buttons (seven evenly spaced on each lapel). Yellow/buff waistcoat with blue border, yellow/buff breeches. A portrait of Captain Pieter Bouwens shows gold domed buttons with a cross, eight on each lapel, which have white piping. Waistbelt is decorated with broad gold lace. Orange sash is worn over the left shoulder.

1766: the coat no longer has lapels, but dark blue Swedish style cuffs and ditto falling collar. In 1770, the falling collar is discontinued, the lapels return (six buttons each).

1772: white coat lined white, with dark blue Swedish style cuffs and falling collar; the coat has no buttons (except for a button for the shoulder strap, hidden under the falling collar), but closes with hooks and eyes. Dark blue waistcoat, yellow/buff breeches. The coat and waistcoat have broad white/dark blue chequered lace along the front, the turnbacks, the cuffs, and on the shoulder strap; the lace is also added to the bandoliers for the carbine and the cartridge box, and on the *sabretache,* the latter bearing in yellow the cypher of Stadtholder Willem V. Housing and holster covers dark blue with yellow lace.

In 1765, Stadtholder Willem V became *inhaber* of the Carabineer Regiment, which was then also elevated to Life Guard status (see Chapter 9).

7

Line Cavalry Regiments

The line regiments made up the bulk of the cavalry arm. Dressed in blue, grey, and white, the regiments were distinguished by linings, cuffs, collars, housing and holster covers in the regimental colour, and again, many regiments opted for red. After 1752, all cavalry regiments were dressed in white. Since it can be difficult to trace the lineage of the different regiments, a letter combination in brackets is added with each regiment for clarification.

(CA) Regiment Van der Duyn, raised 1577 as Lancer Company Melun (Holland establishment).

After being transformed to Horse (1597) and Cuirassiers (1604), it became the *Garde te Paard van Zijne Hoogheid* (His Highness' Horse Guards) in 1625, and in 1647 the *Regiment Gardes te Paard van de Staten van Holland* (The States of Hollands' Horse Guards Regiment). It lost its guard status in 1673.

Inhaber from 1707 Van der Duyn van 's-Gravemoer, 1728 Schack.

In 1720, incorporated Erbach's Regiment (CT) as 2nd squadron. In 1749, became 3rd and 4th squadrons of Buys' Regiment (CR).

Battles: Fontenoy, Rocoux, Lauffeld.

Uniform during the 1720s and 1730s according to a reconstruction by Hoynck van Papendrecht white coat lined red, with red full cuffs, brass buttons. Red waistcoat and breeches. Red housing and holster covers. Officers have hats with white ostrich plumes and gold lace, and two rows of gold lace on the housing and holster covers.

1739: waistcoat and breeches are buff. Trumpeters have red coats lined white, with white cuffs, gold buttons; a receipt includes 700 ells gold lace for trumpeters; 20 ells silver lace for NCOs.

1743: portrait of Lieutenant Steenhard shows white coat lined light blue, with light blue full cuffs, lapels and falling collar, silver domed buttons (eight on each lapel). White waistcoat visible under cuirass.

1748: white coat lined light blue, with light blue Swedish cuffs, squared off lapels and shoulder strap, pewter buttons. Yellow/buff waistcoat and breeches.

(CB) Regiment Van Rechteren, raised 1585 as Horse Company Van Nieuwenaar en Meurs (Zeeland establishment).

Disbanded in 1668, re-raised in 1672; in 1747 became 2nd squadron of the Regiment Nassau-La Leq (CE).

Inhaber from 1708 Van Rechteren van Noorddeuringen, 1739 Moenen, 1741 Van Rechteren, sometimes mentioned as Rechteren-Zeeland.

Battles: Rocoux.

Uniform in 1730–1740 is white with red, presumably pewter buttons; buff waistcoat and breeches; red housing and holster covers with white lace. Receipt from 1741 mentions that the uniform 'remains as it is now, except the buttons need to be ordered larger. The trumpeters' dress red and yellow, but with different [livery] cords, and laced differently. The *banderollen* yellow'.

(CC) Regiment Van Oyen, raised 1588 as Harqebusier Company Marcelis Bacx (Establishment unknown).

Inhaber from 1706 Van Oyen. In 1720 became 2nd squadron of Rechterens' regiment (CP) .

(CD) Regiment Van Pritzelwitz, raised 1588 as Lancer Company Paulus Bacx (Holland establishment).

From 1708 Van Pritzelwitz. In 1725 became 2nd squadron of Cralingen's Regiment (CQ).

(CE) Regiment Graaf Maurits van Nassau, raised 1599 as Horse Company De la Salle (Zeeland establishment).

Also known as Regiment La Lecq. In 1648 elevated to guard status, designated *Garde te Paard van de Staten van Zeeland* (States of Zeelands' Horse Guards)in 1660, then *Garde te Paard van Zijne Hoogheid* (His Highness' Horse Guards); also known as *Guardes du Corps van Zeeland*. Lost its guard status in 1705.

Inhaber from 1708 Willem Maurits Count Nassau-La Lecq.

In 1747, incorporated Van Rechteren-Zeeland's Regiment (CB) as 2nd squadron. In 1752 became 3rd and 4th squadron of Van Nassau-Beverweerd's Regiment (CS), but remained on the Zeeland establishment.

Battles: Germany, Fontenoy, siege of Brussels, Rocoux, Lauffeld.

Uniform around 1700: red coat lined red, with blue full cuffs, gold buttons; hats with gold lace; housing and holster covers red. Officers have plumes on the hats, lace and embroidery on the housing and holster covers. Trumpeters as the troopers, but with *banderollen* and heavily decorated with gold lace, plumes on the hats; trumpet banners and standard blue.

In 1743, the uniform is depicted as blue with red.

(CF) Regiment Hessen-Homburg, raised 1599 as Horse Company Van Randwijk van Gameren (Groningen establishment).

Inhaber from 1692 van Hessen-Homburg, 1748 van Lintelo. Disbanded in 1749.

Battles: Fontenoy.

A painting by Troost, dated 1742, gives a good impression of the uniforms and appearance of this regiment: dark blue coat lined poppy red, with red round cuffs, lapels and falling collar, dark blue cuff flap, pewter buttons (four on the cuff flaps, seven on the lapels). Yellow waistcoat and breeches. Hat with silver lace and black cockade. Black neck stock. Carbine belt of buff/yellow leather with silver lace trim. Blue housing and holster covers with what appears to be narrow white lace and embroidery.

Officers' coats have full cuffs but no lapels or collar; heavy silver lace and embroidery along the front and on the cuffs, as well as on the waistcoat, silver lace on the outer seams of the breeches; hats with silver lace; all buttons silver; white neck stocks.

Trumpeters are dressed in livery colours, viz. dark grey coat lined light blue, but no cuffs, collar or lapels. Light blue waistcoat with silver lace decoration, yellow/buff breeches with silver lace on outer seams. Hat with silver lace and black cockade. White neck stocks with silver buckle. Blue housing and holster covers with silver lace, embroidery and fringe. Silver trumpets with cords and tassels.

The kettledrummer is a man of colour, wearing a dark blue coat lined red, no cuffs, collar or lapels, but decorated with silver lace. Red waistcoat with silver lace along the front and the pocket flaps, yellow/buff breeches with silver lace on the outer seams. White turban with gold cord and black ostrich feather. Silver slave collar. Housing red with silver lace, kettledrums have dark blue covers with silver(?) cords, tassels and fringe.

(CG) Regiment Van Saksen-Heilburg, raised 1625 as Cuirassier Company Caumont de Force (Holland establishment).

Inhaber from 1693 van Saksen-Heilburg.

In 1716, incorporated Chanclos' Regiment (CU) as 2nd squadron. In 1723 became 2nd squadron of Van Bentheim's Regiment (CM).

(CH) Regiment Ginkel, raised 1625 as Cuirassier Company De la Tour d'Auvergne (Utrecht establishment).

Inhaber from 1709 Van Reede van Ginkel en Lievendaal, 1747 van Isendoorn à Bloys van Cannenburg.

In 1771 became the 3rd and 4th squadrons of Van Eck's Regiment (CL), but remained on the Utrecht establishment.

Battles: Fontenoy, Rocoux, Lauffeld.

Uniform in the 1730s-1740s white lined red with red narrow cuffs, white cuff flaps, red lapels, pewter buttons; yellow/buff waistcoat and breeches; hat with false silver lace; red housing and pistol covers, with white lace edge.

Portrait of Colonel Van Reede Ginkel, dated probably 1730–1740, shows a white coat lined poppy red, with poppy red narrow cuffs, white cuff flaps, poppy red lapels, silver domed buttons; silver floral lace around the cuffs and lapels, and as straight lace loops around the buttonholes of the cuff flaps, lapels (in pairs) and pocket flaps. Yellow/buff waistcoat lined yellow/buff, with silver lace around the edges of the lining, which becomes visible because the corners are hooked together; yellow/buff breeches. Orange sash around the waist. Silver sword knot with silver tassel.

Posthumous portrait of Colonel Johan Hendrik Isendoorn à Blois (*inhaber* in 1703, killed that same year during an action at Ekeren), shows red housing and holster covers with silver fringe and heavy silver floral embroidery; also in natural colours a coat of arms, above that an emblem of a harness and helmet, flanked by standards, over crossed gun barrels and a stack of cannonball; the emblem of the harness *et al* copied on the holster covers.

Portrait of Colonel Frederik Johan van Isendoorn à Bloys, dated probably 1740–1745 (and which is nearly identical to that of Colonel Van Reede Ginkel) shows a similar uniform, but the cuffs, cuff flaps and lapels are slightly more narrow, buttons are somewhat smaller; the coat is decorated with silver floral embroidery along the edges of the cuffs, cuff flaps, lapels, pocket flaps and the front of the coat. Broad silver lace along the edge of the lining of the yellow/buff waistcoat (again turned up), two rows of lace around the pocket flaps; orange sash around the waist, silver with red intertwined sword knot with silver and red tassel.

1753–1771: the uniform for this unit remained practically the same, with perhaps only minor changes to the cut, according to the fashion of the day: white coat lined red with red Swedish style cuffs and red small standing collar (white in 1766), white shoulder strap piped red, pewter buttons (seven evenly spaced on each lapel). Yellow/buff waistcoat with red border, yellow/buff breeches.

(CI) Regiment Wassenaar, raised 1645 as Regiment Van den Berg (Holland establishment).

Inhaber from 1672 Van Wassenaer van Obdam en Voorschoten, 1715 van Pallandt.

In 1730 became 2nd squadron of Van Nassau-Beverweerd's Regiment (CS).

(CK) Regiment Hesse-Cassel, raised 1665 as Regiment Catzler (Holland establishment).

Inhaber from 1710 Frederick Prince of Hesse-Cassel, 1721 Prince of Hessen-Phillipsthal.

In 1761 became 4th squadron of Buys' Regiment (CR).

Battles: Siege of Menin (2nd squadron), Siege of Ypres (3rd squadron), Rocoux, Lauffeld.

Uniform in 1730–1740 white coat lined light blue, with full light blue cuffs, pewter buttons. Light blue waistcoat, buff breeches. Housing and holster covers light blue with white lace edge. Officers have gold aiguillettes and gold lace on the housing and holster covers.

1740s: the waistcoat and breeches change to yellow. Trumpeters wear a blue coat lined red, with red cuffs, gilded buttons, also yellow smallclothes. Hat has gold lace. Portrait of the colonel-commander Major General Count Van Rechteren, dated 1748 or later, shows white coat lined sky blue, with narrow sky blue cuffs, domed silver buttons; silver floral embroidery along buttons and buttonholes. Yellow waistcoat with silver lace, yellow breeches. Orange sash around the waist.

1753: white coat lined light blue, with light blue narrow cuffs and lapels, white small standing collar, pewter buttons. Yellow waistcoat and breeches.

Portrait of Frederik Willem Count Rechteren, Hessen-Phillipsthal's regiment, 1760. (Stichting Collectie Van Rechteren-Limpurg, with kind permission by Mr N. Count Van Rechteren)

(CL) Regiment Van Reede-Aughrim, raised 1665 as Regiment Van Rechteren (Gelderland establishment). Disbanded in 1668, but re-raised in 1671.

Inhaber from 1696 Van Reede Baron Aughrim, 1719 Van Lynden van der Parck, 1735 Van Keppel, 1740 Van Lynden tot Blitterswijk, 1747 van Eck van Nergena.

In 1771, incorporated Cannenburg's Regiment (CH) as 3rd and 4th squadrons. In 1795, the regiment was incorporated into the *2e Regiment Zware Cavalerie.*

Battles: Fontenoy, Rocoux, Lauffeld.

Uniform around 1700: grey coat lined blue, with blue full cuffs. Red housing and holster covers. Trumpeters wear red coats with gold lace on the sleeves and red *banderollen* on the back.

1740s: white coat lined red, with red full cuffs, pewter buttons. Yellow/buff waistcoat and breeches. Red housing and holster covers with white lace edge. Trumpeters (presumably) wore a green coat lined red, with red full cuffs, silver buttons (based on the Van Eck van Nergena coat of arms). Portrait of Colonel Van Eck van Nergena dated 1747 shows white coat lined red, with red narrow cuffs and lapels, silver buttons. Yellow/buff waistcoat.

In the latter half of the 18th century, the uniform remained white with red; trumpeters as the troopers, but with small white 'swallows' nests' and *banderollen*. In 1772, the coat had straight cuffs, a white small standing collar, white shoulder strap piped red, pewter buttons.

(CM) Regiment Tilly, raised 1671 as Regiment Van den Boetzelaar (Holland establishment).

Inhaber from 1680 Tserclaes van Tilly, 1723 Van Bentheim, 1734 Van Lynden, 1741 Le Sans de Sandouville, 1745 Van Birkenfeld.

In 1714, incorporated part of Georgin's Regiment (CV). In 1723, incorporated the Regiment Van Saksen-Heilburg (CG) as 2nd and 3rd squadrons. In 1760, the regiment became the 3rd and 4th squadrons of Heinenoord's Regiment (CQ).

Battles: Fontenoy, Rocoux, Lauffeldt.

Uniform in 1732: white coat lined red, with red full cuffs, pewter buttons. Officers have silver buttons and silver lace decorations. In 1746, the uniform is described as being similar to that of the Austrian Cuirassier Regiment Birkenfeld (*Kürassierregiment* K10), 'except for the cuirasses'; this suggests a red falling collar. Hat is described as having white lace. Smallclothes most likely yellow/buff instead of red. Red housing and holster covers with white lace edge.

1753: coat has red Swedish cuffs and red small standing collar. Yellow waistcoat and breeches.

(CN) Regiment Van Eck, raised 1671 as Regiment Nassau-Saarbrücken (Holland establishment).

Inhaber from 1702 Van Eck. In 1714, incorporated part of Georgin's Regiment (CV). In 1719, became 2nd squadron of Drymborn's Regiment (CR).

(CO) Regiment Van Vittinghof, raised 1672 as Regiment Brempt (Overijssel establishment).

Inhaber from 1692 Van Vittinghof Scheel van Nederhemert, 1726 Van Haersolte tot Herxen, 1746 Van Rechteren (Rechteren-Overijssel).

In 1762, incorporated Hop's Regiment (CP) as 3rd and 4th squadrons. In 1795, the regiment was incorporated into the *2e Regiment Zware Cavalerie*.

Battles: Germany, Fontenoy, Rocoux, Lauffeld.

Portrait of J.R.B.R. Count Rechteren, *ritmeester* in Rechterens' Regiment, 1749. (Stichting Collectie Van Rechteren-Limpurg, with kind permission by Mr N. Count Van Rechteren)

Uniform from 1740–1748: grey-white coat lined yellow, with yellow cuffs, pewter buttons. Trumpeters probably in red with yellow from 1746, like Van Rechteren-Zeeland's regiment (CB). Buff/yellow waistcoat and breeches. Yellow housing and holster covers with white lace. From 1749, the uniforms are white with red.

1758: children's portrait of F.L.C. van Rechteren shows white coat lined red, with red narrow cuffs and white cuff flaps, red lapels, red falling collar, brass buttons. Yellow waistcoat and breeches. Hat with gold lace.

Around 1766: a red aiguillette on the right shoulder is added; each lapel has nine buttons, grouped 3 x 3. Buff coloured waistcoat and breeches.

In 1771, the top of the lapel buttons over the collar on the front; the buttons on each lapel are evenly spaced. Portrait of Captain W.T. Nobel shows hat with gold lace and black cockade, red housing and holster covers with two rows of gold lace.

(CP) Regiment Van Rechteren, raised 1672 as Regiment Stoltzenberg (Holland establishment).

Inhaber from 1710 Van Rechteren, 1742 Hop.

In 1720, incorporated Hoeufft van Oyen's Regiment (CC) as 2nd squadron. In 1762, the regiment became 3rd and 4th squadrons of Rechteren's Regiment (CO), but remained on the Holland establishment.

Battles: Germany.

Uniform depicted in 1743 as white with red. From 1744, trumpeters wear livery lace on the coats, 700 ells being delivered that year; the receipt also lists gold lace, 290 aiguillettes and sword knots.

1753: white coat lined red, with red narrow cuffs and red cuff flaps, lapels and small standing collar, brass buttons. Yellow/buff waistcoat and breeches.

(CQ) Regiment Cralingen, raised 1672 as Regiment Van Welle (Holland establishment).

Inhaber from 1701 Du Faget van Assendelft lord Cralingen en Heinenoord, 1732 De Boncour, 1737 Schultz van Hagen, 1748 Du Faget van Assendelft lord Heinenoord en Besoyen, 1763 De Famars.

In 1726, incorporated Van Pritzelwitz's Regiment (CD) as 2nd squadron. In 1760, the 3rd squadron is disbanded, after which Birkenfeld's Regiment (CM) is incorporated as the 3rd and 4th squadrons. In 1795, became the *1e Regiment Zware Cavalerie.*

Battles: Rocoux, Lauffeld.

Uniform from 1737 white coat lined dark green, with dark green large full cuffs, brass buttons; yellow/buff waistcoat and breeches. Dark green housing and holster covers with yellow lace edge (gold for officers). A group portrait, dated around 1741, shows Sous-Lieutenant F.C.W.L. Count Van Bylandt in this uniform, with gold buttons and gold floral embroidered loops on the buttons on the front (grouped 1-2-3) and on the cuffs. Buff/yellow waistcoat with gold lace edge, buff/yellow breeches. Orange sash over the right shoulder. White cravat. An officer dressed similarly can be seen in a print of the funeral procession of Willem IV in 1752.

1753: white coat lined dark green, with dark green Swedish cuffs and squared off lapels, white small standing collar, white shoulder strap edged dark green, brass buttons. Seven buttons evenly spaced on each lapel. Yellow/buff waistcoat and breeches.

Frederik Reinhard Burchard Rudolf, aged 7, dressed in the uniform of Van Rechterens' Cavalry Regiment, 1758. (Stichting Collectie Van Rechteren-Limpurg, with kind permission by Mr N. Count Van Rechteren)

1763(?): white coat lined white, with black straight cuffs and falling collar, black shoulder straps with red fringe, brass buttons.

1767: buttons now pewter; the red fringe is discontinued.

1771: white coat lined poppy red, with black straight cuffs, lapels, falling collar and shoulder strap, pewter buttons (six evenly spaced on each lapel, two on the cuffs). Yellow/buff waistcoat and breeches. Red housing and holster covers with white lace edge. Except for some minor changes, this uniform was worn until 1806, being adopted after 1795 as the uniform for the *1e Regiment Zware Cavalerie* of the Batavian Republic.

(CR) Regiment Van Drymborn, raised 1672 as Regiment Van Flodorff (Holland establishment).

Inhaber from 1704 Lieutenant General Baron Van Drymborn, 1724 Baron Van Drymborn, 1738 Van Son, 1740 Buys.

In 1719, incorporated Van Eck's Regiment (CN) as 2nd squadron. In 1751, incorporated Schacks' Regiment (A) as 3rd and 4th squadrons. In 1761, the 4th squadron is disbanded, after which Hessen-Phillipsthal's Regiment (CK)

Paulus Hubert Buys (1707–1775), colonel-proprietor of a cavalry regiment; portrait by Albertus Frese jr., dated 1745. (Stichting Kasteel Loenersloot, De Bilt)

is incorporated as 4th squadron. In 1795, the regiment is incorporated into the *1e Regiment Zware Cavalerie*.

Battles: Fontenoy, Rocoux, Lauffeld.

Uniform around 1730 is a grey/white coat lined red, with red large full cuffs. Grey/white waistcoat and breeches. Red housing and holster covers.

1743: receipt for white and red broadcloth and pewter buttons; portrait of Colonel Buys dated 1745 shows white coat lined red, with red full cuffs and red narrow lapels, silver domed buttons; the lapels rounded off at the bottom, each with ten evenly spaced buttons. Yellow/buff waistcoat with silver lace decoration along the edges and pocket flaps, yellow/buff breeches. Hat with broad silver lace and black ostrich plumes, narrow silver lace loop, silver button and black cockade. Orange sash around the waist. Silver lace on the waistbelt.

1748: a receipt mentions greyish white cloth and madder red baize for troopers' coats, and 'buff coat coloured' cloth for smallclothes. Also '2½ lbs white and buff coat coloured worsted lace' for lace loops on the coat and waistcoat. Large and small tinned copper buttons. NCOs have uniforms of finer broadcloth. Also listed is red cloth for housing and holster covers; for the NCOs of cloth of finer quality, with broad silver lace. Trumpeters and kettledrummer wear poppy red coats lined white, with white cuffs; coat is decorated with broad and narrow silk livery lace and gilded buttons. Yellow/buff smallclothes.

1752: white coat lined red, with red Swedish cuffs and squared off lapels, brass buttons (seven on each lapel); yellow aiguillettes on the right shoulder. Yellow/buff waistcoat and breeches. A portrait of colonel-commander Van Eck van Overbeek shows the lapels with eight buttons in pairs.

From around 1766 until 1773, the coat has straight cuffs, narrow squared off lapels, falling collar and white shoulder strap edged red.

(CS) Regiment Nassau-La Lecq, raised 1688 as Regiment Van der Duyn (Holland establishment).

Inhaber from 1698 Maurits Lodewijk Count Nassau-La Lecq, 1741 Otto, 1742 Schagen, 1749 Willem Hendrik Count Nassau-La Lecq lord Beverweerd, 1763 Van der Beke, 1768 Stavenisse-Pous.

In 1729, incorporated Palland's regiment (CI) as 2nd squadron. In 1752, incorporated the Regiment Nassau-La Lecq (CE) as 3rd and 4th squadron; in 1763, the 1st and 2nd squadron switch to the Zeeland establishment, while 3rd and 4th switch to the Holland establishment. In 1795, the regiment is incorporated into the *1e Regiment Zware Cavalerie*.

Battles: Rocoux, Lauffeld.

Uniform from 1753 to 1767 is a white coat lined red, with red Swedish style cuff and red lapels that go along the length of the coat, white shoulder strap edged red, red piping along the pocket flaps, white small standing collar, brass buttons. Yellow/buff waistcoat with red edge along the front, yellow/buff breeches; on the cuff of the coat a yellow/buff narrow false turned back sleeve. The long lapels, with 13 buttons, are a regimental feature, repeated until 1768. The facing colour changes to dark blue around 1760, lapels have 14 buttons each.

1764: the dark blue Swedish style cuffs become more narrow, the false yellow/buff turnback cuff disappears, as well as the dark blue edge on the waistcoat; the dark blue lapels along the front of the coat have 15 buttons.

1766: buttons now pewter (13 on the lapels); waistcoat and breeches dark blue.

1768: white coat lined dark blue, with dark blue narrow Swedish cuffs, dark blue falling collar, white shoulder straps edged dark blue, pewter buttons. Dark blue waistcoat and breeches.

1770: a portrait of Colonel De Jongh, *inhaber* of the 3rd company, shows white coat lined red, with red round cuffs, silver domed buttons (seven visible on each side along the front); buff falling collar with broad silver lace, on the cuffs a buff false turned up cuff with broad silver lace edge. Silver aiguillettes, the cords braided into an epaulette, on the right shoulder, with the rest falling halfway the upper arm. Buff waistcoat with broad silver lace along the edges and pocket flaps. Orange sash around the waist. Black cravat. Sabre with iron hilt. The *Jassenboekje* shows the same uniform, with 10 buttons in pairs on each side on the front, a red shoulder strap with green fringe, and a red edge on the waistcoat.

1772: the false turned up buff cuffs and buff collar are discontinued; instead a red narrow Swedish cuff and red falling collar; the shoulder strap without fringe.

(CT) **Regiment Van Erbach**, raised 1688 as Regiment Van Erffa (Establishment unknown).

Inhaber from 1692 Van Erbach. In 1720 became 2nd squadron of Van der Duyn's Regiment (CA).

(CU) **Regiment De Chanclos**, raised 1693 as Regiment De Chauviry (Establishment unknown).

Inhaber from 1701 De Chanclos de Rets Brisuila. In 1716 became 2nd squadron in Saksen-Heilburg's Regiment (CG).

(CV) **Regiment De Georgin**, raised 1693 as Regiment De Grisperre (Establishment unknown).

Inhaber from 1710 De Georgin. In 1714 divided between Regiments De Tilly (CM) and Van Eck (CN).

(CW) **Regiment Van Glinstra**, raised 1701 as Regiment Van Eminga (Friesland establishment).

Inhaber from 1706 Van Glinstra. Disbanded in 1714.

(CX) Regiment Sirtema van Grovestins, raised 1701 (Friesland establishment)

Disbanded in 1714.

(CY) Regiment Van Voorst, raised 1701 as Regiment De Baldwin (Establishment unknown).

Inhaber from 1710 Van Voorst. Disbanded in 1715.

8

Dragoons

The first two dragoon regiments, each 1,000 men strong, were raised in 1672 by Frederick Casimir Count of Courland and Semigallia (present day Latvia); they are depicted in a print of the Siege of Naarden from 1673, sporting fur caps with red bags, and wild moustaches. The first regiment became the Guard Dragoon Regiment (see chapter 6). Other dragoon regiments followed in 1688 and 1693. All regiments were placed on the Holland establishment. Already during the War of the Spanish Succession, the dragoons were regarded as cavalry, although after the war, the regiments were dismounted; Schlippenbach's Regiment was deployed as infantry in England in 1715. In 1726, the regiments were again mounted. They retained certain infantry features, such as the ranks of ensign and sergeant, mounted drummers, and a drum major. During the first half of the 18th century, all dragoons were dressed in dark blue and red (except the Saxe-Gotha Regiment), with pewter buttons; the housing was red with a white lace edge for all regiments. Different regimental colours for cuffs, collars and lapels appeared after 1769. The remaining two regiments, Hesse-Cassel's and Bylandt's, were reorganised into one Dragoon Regiment in 1795.

Regiment Dragonders Schlippenbach, raised 1672 as *Regiment Dragonders* Brandt.

Inhaber from 1693 Major General Christoper III van Schlippenbach, 1715 Van der Duyn, 1737 Lieutenant General Casimir Abraham van Schlippenbach, 1750 Ditfourth

In 1752, the regiment was incorporated into the regiments Massau and Berg van Trips.

Battles: England (1715), Germany, Fontenoy, Rocoux, Lauffeld.

Little is known about the uniforms before 1730, but Casimir Abraham van Schlippenbach gives some information in his memoirs. In 1711, he obtained permission by the Council of State to raise a grenadier company; for this company, he ordered embroidered grenadier caps and cartridge boxes. The caps had in all probability his coat of arms on the front flap, since he was made count that year by the Habsburg claimant Charles III (Emperor Charles IV). The coat of arms is quartered, with a tower in the 1st and 4th quarter, and an arm in armour holding a sword in the 2nd and 3rd; at the centre the family crest, being a yellow chain on a black ground. The shield is crowned with a count's crown, and flanked by a griffon on the left and a lion on the right, both holding a banner. The little flap might have borne his name, a motto, or 'Hollandia'. The flaps of the cartridge boxes were probably embroidered with a monogram. The grenadiers were selected from the line companies, and rode black horses. The company was disbanded in 1741.

1731: blue coat lined red with full red cuffs, the buttonholes with white worsted lace loops and a white woollen fringed epaulette; officers' coats have buttonholes and epaulettes worked with silver thread. A group portrait dated 1741 shows Lieutenant O.J.C. Count Van Bylandt in a dark blue coat lined red, with red full cuffs and dark blue cuff flaps, red lapels, silver buttons; silver straight lace loops with tassels (three on each cuff flap, pocket flap and below each lapel, 10 on each lapel). Yellow/buff waistcoat with silver broad lace along the front, yellow/buff breeches. Orange sash around the waist. White cravat.

Regiment Dragonders Van Dopf, raised 1688 as *Regiment Dragonders* Van Berlo.

Inhaber from 1693 Van Dopf, 1718 Chalmot du Portail, 1736 van Heylman, 1742 van Massau, 1757 Ditfourth, 1768 van Hessen-Kassel.

In 1752, incorporated part of Schlippenbach's Regiment as 2nd squadron.

Battles: Germany, Fontenoy, Rocoux, Hulst, Lauffeld.

Uniform during the 1740s is a coat with full cuffs and lapels. Yellow/buff waistcoat and breeches.

1753: coat with Swedish cuffs, lapels and dark blue small standing collar.

1763: coat has Swedish cuffs, red falling collar, dark blue shoulder strap; white straight lace loops along the front (10 pairs evenly spaced) and on the cuffs and pocket flaps, dark blue shoulder strap with white lace edge.

1766: ditto, but blue waistcoat with straight white lace loops along the front and on the pocket flaps (three each); on the right shoulder a dark blue shoulder strap with white lace decoration and white fringe.

1769: coat lined red, with yellow straight cuffs, squared off lapels and falling collar, dark blue shoulder strap edged yellow; white straight lace loops on the lapels (six on each, in pairs), below the lapels (two pairs), on the cuffs and pocket flaps (three each), and one on the shoulder strap. Yellow waistcoat and breeches. In 1772, the colour of the cuffs (now closing vertically with two small buttons), lapels and collar changes to pink.

Regiment Dragonders Van Wassenaar (Walloon), raised 1693 as *Regiment Dragonders* Mattha.

From 1711 Van Wassenaar, 1733 Mattha, 1748 Berg van Trips, 1768 Van Bylandt.

In 1752, incorporated part of Schlippenbach's Regiment as 2nd squadron.

Battles: Germany, Rocoux, Hulst, Lauffeld, Bergen op Zoom.

Little is known about the earlier uniforms; a full length portrait by Tibout Regters, dated 1748, shows the painter Ludolf Bakhuyzen II in full uniform, viz. dark blue coat lined red, with red full cuffs and dark blue small standing collar; buttons are pewter (silver?), with silver embroidered

Ludolf Bakhuyzen II, in the uniform of a dragoon of Trips' Regiment, by T. Regters, 1748. (Rijksmuseum)

buttonholes. Yellow waistcoat with silver lace along the front and the pocket flaps. Hat with silver lace, a narrow silver lace loop and button, orange cockade. White cravat. High riding boots, white linen protective knee covers, attached to what appears to be the cloth-covered buttons of the breeches. Bakhuyzen wears dark blue or black breeches; he carries a decorative sword with orange sword knot on a buff leather waist belt under the waistcoat. The cockade and sword knot are most likely an expression of loyalty to Stadtholder Prince Willem IV.

1753: coat has Swedish cuffs and small dark blue standing collar; this is the only dragoon regiment without lapels on the coat.

1763–1768: coat has Swedish cuffs, dark blue standing collar, dark blue shoulder strap; white straight lace loops along the front (10 pairs evenly spaced) and on the cuffs and pocket flaps (three each), and one on a red ground on the collar, white lace edge on the shoulder strap.

1769: coat lined red, with pink straight cuffs, squared off lapels and falling collar; no lace, except on the dark blue shoulder strap . Yellow waistcoat and breeches. In 1772, the cuffs close vertically with four small buttons (two on the cuff, two above), two buttons are added below the lapels, shoulder straps are dark blue with white lace edge and white wool fringe.

Regiment Dragonders Saxe-Gotha (German), raised 1745.
Inhaber from 1745 Friedrich III Herzog von Saxe-Gotha-Altenburg.

The regiment was taken into service as part of a corps hired from the Duke of Saxe-Gotha-Altenburg, and was discharged from service after 1748.

Battles: Rocourt, Hulst, Lauffeld.

Uniform: white coat lined red, with red Swedish style cuffs and falling collar, white shoulder flap edged red, pewter buttons. Red waistcoat and breeches. Hat edged with white lace. Housing, holster covers and portmanteau red with white lace edge.

Regiment Waalse Dragonders Cornabé (Walloon), raised 1747.
Inhaber from 1747 Cornabé, 1752 Lillers.

Raised in April 1747 as a dragoon regiment as part of 'Cornabé's Legion' (Chapter 9), but designated as infantry two months later. In 1762, the regiment became the 2nd battalion of the *Regiment Walen* Smissaert (see Part 1 for more information).

Uniform (presumably) like that of Trips' Regiment (see Regiment Dragonders Van Wassenaar).

Regiment Dragonders d'Olne (Walloon), raised 1747.
Inhaber from 1747 d'Olne de Saint Hallier.

The regiment was disbanded in 1749.

Uniform (presumably) like that of Trips' Regiment (see Regiment Dragonders Van Wassenaar); a watercolour in the Vinkhuijzen collection shows red waistcoat and breeches.

9

Light Cavalry: Carabineers, Hussars and Free Corps

The light cavalry element in the first half of the 18th century was formed by the Regiment Karabiniers (Carabineer Regiment). Only one regiment was raised and titled as such, placed on the Holland establishment. It is said to have been combined in 1765 with the *Oranje-Friesland* Life Guard Regiment to form one regiment of four squadrons, though both units are mentioned separately in all contemporary sources, and wore distinctive uniforms; the Carabineers also remained on the Holland establishment. The only distinctive feature was the softer riding boots they wore, instead of the high, stiff cavalry boots of the line cavalry. In a few cases, they fought on foot like the dragoons.

During the War of the Austrian Succession, independent 'free companies' of dragoons and hussars were raised for the duration of the war, often in combination with infantry companies, to act as irregular cavalry. Many of these were raised by Protestant French officers and recruited among French prisoners and deserters. Snouckaert van Schauburg shows Haiduks and Hussars from 1703 in his work on Dutch hussars throughout the centuries, and a watercolour in the Vinkhuijzen Collection shows a hussar from a corps, allegedly in service from April 1706 to November 1709. So far, these are the only sources for the existence of hussars in the States' army before the Bavarian regiment of Count Frangipani was taken into service in 1744. From this regiment, two other regiments would be formed, but the war was over before these, and other regiments and free corps, were ready. Except for Cornabé's Legion, none saw any action. All free companies and hussars were on the Holland establishment. The last hussars would disappear from the army after the reorganisation of 1752, only to reappear once again as free corps cavalry in 1784.

Regiment Karabiniers Van Lynden, raised 1688 as *Regiment Karabiniers* Lippe.

Inhaber from 1694 Van Keppel van Albemarle, 1718 Van Lynden van Leeuwenberg, 1728 Van der Gronden , 1735 Hoefft van Oyen, 1765 Willem V of Orange-Nassau; the regiment received the status of a Life Guard regiment and was renamed *Oranje Carabiniers* or *Carabiniers van Syne Hoogheid.* In

1795, it was incorporated together with the *Regiment Oranje-Friesland* into the *2e Regiment Zware Cavalerie*.

Battles: Germany, Fontenoy, siege of Brussels, Rocoux, Lauffeld.

Uniform is depicted in 1743 as white with red.

1748: grey coat lined red, with red Swedish style cuffs and red lapels, grey small standing collar, grey shoulder flap with red piping, brass buttons (seven evenly spaced on each lapel). Yellow/buff waistcoat with red border, yellow/buff breeches. Trumpeters wear a blue coat lined red, with red Swedish cuffs, brass buttons; coat is decorated with black and white livery cord and lace. Yellow/buff waistcoat and breeches.

1760(?): as above, but coat is white with blue. The uniform in the 1760s closely resembles that of the *Oranje-Friesland* Life Guard Regiment, except for the waistcoat, which has no blue border (see description of that regiment). The *Jassenboekje* shows the same shade of blue for both regiments, but other illustrations, like those of Macalaster Loup, and later Coopman, show the Carabineers as having light blue facings, as opposed to the dark blue facing colour of the Lifeguards.

Officer of Frangipani's Hussars, 1748, after Schnouckart van Schauburg. (Vinkhuijzen Collection)

1771: white coat lined light blue, with light blue straight cuff and lapels, white small standing collar, white shoulder strap with light blue piping, brass buttons (three on each cuff, six in pairs on each lapel). Cuff closes vertically with four small buttons (two above- and two on the cuff). Yellow/buff smallclothes. Hat with black cockade and white plume, no lace edge. Housing and holster covers yellow, with white lace.

Regiment Huzaren Frangipani, raised 1744, taken into service in 1745.

Inhaber from 1744 Gregoire Count Frangipani.

The regiment consisted of eight companies, organised into four squadrons. In 1748, the regiment was disbanded and divided between Collignon's Regiment (two companies) and Sandor's Corps (six companies), both regiments however existed only on paper and were soon disbanded.

Battles: Siege of Brussels, Lauffeld, Bergen op Zoom.

One source suggests the Bavarian uniform was yellow and dark blue, but so far, no confirmation of this has been found. According to a reconstruction by Snouckaert van Schauburg, the uniform consisted of a red dolman with yellow cords and tassels and yellow lace, brass buttons. Red charivaris with yellow Austrian knots and decorative embroidery on the seams of the lower leg. Green pelisse with dark brown fur. Dark brown fur colpack with green hanging bag and a sprig of feathers on the left side. Yellow *sabretache* with a red rampant lion. Housing is red with dark green toothed edge with yellow cord along the edges, and a crowned yellow rampant lion emblem in the corners. Officers all cords and lace gold instead of yellow, yellow leather gloves and yellow leather boots; housing with gold embroidered emblems and gold braid, broad gold lace edge with two thin dark green lines.

Vrij Compagniën Dragonders (Free Companies of Dragoons)

Company of Captain Bignon, raised 1745 (with infantry company of the same commander).

Company of Captain Van Hördt, raised 1745 with infantry company of Captain-Lieutenant Roodt (See part 1 for more information).

Battles: Lauffeld, Bergen op Zoom

There is no information about the uniforms, although it is very likely these companies wore dark blue uniforms with different coloured lining, cuffs, and lapels, like their infantry counterparts.

Legioen van Cornabé (Cornabé's Legion), raised 1747.

One company of Dragoons.

One company of Hussars.

Both companies were disbanded in 1748.

Battles: Lauffeld.

Regiment Huzaren van de Staat (State's Hussars), raised 1748.

Inhaber from 1748 De Zigrai (Michael Zsigray), 1749 Sándor (30 January–30 April), -?

The regiment was disbanded in 1752.

In all probability, these 'State's Hussars' or 'National Hussars' wore uniforms similar to those of Frangipani's Regiment. A hussar officer depicted in a print of the funeral procession of Willem IV wears a green uniform with gold cords and buttons, but this is likely due to the imagination of the colourist.

Regiment Huzaren Collignon, raised 1748.

Inhaber from 1748 De Collignon.

The regiment was formed by two companies of Frangipani's Regiment, but never fully organised.

Korps Sandor, raised 1748.

Inhaber from 1748 Sándor.

The corps, consisting of dragoons and hussars, was formed by six companies of Frangipani's Regiment, but existed only on paper. Colonel Gregor Sándor, a former major in Frangipani's Regiment, took over command of the State's Hussars the next year but retired three months later.

Appendix I

Raadpensionarissen and Stadtholders of the Dutch Republic in the 18th Century

Raadpensionarissen

Anthonie Heinsius	1689–1720
Isaac van Hoornbeek	1720–1727
Simon van Slingelandt	1727–1737
Anthonie van der Heim	1737–1746
Willem Buys	1746
Jacob Gilles	1746–1749
Pieter Steyn	1749–1772

Stadtholders,
– of Friesland

Prince Johan Willem Friso von Nassau-Dietz	1697–1711 (1)
Prince Willem IV van Oranje-Nassau	1711–1751 (2)
Prince Willem V van Oranje-Nassau	1751–1795 (3)

– of Groningen

Prince Johan Willem Friso von Nassau-Dietz	1697–1711
Stadtholderless Era	1711–1718
Prince Willem IV van Oranje-Nassau	1718–1751 (2)
Prince Willem V van Oranje-Nassau	1751–1795 (3)

– of Gelderland and Drenthe

Prince Willem III van Oranje	1696–1702
Stadtholderless Era	1702–1722
Prince Willem IV van Oranje-Nassau	1722–1751 (2)
Prince Willem V van Oranje-Nassau	1751–1795

– of Holland, Zeeland, Utrecht and Overijssel

Prince Willem III van Oranje	1696–1702
Stadtholderless Era	1702–1747
Prince Willem IV van Oranje-Nassau	1747–1751
Prince Willem V van Oranje-Nassau	1751–1795 (3)

Regents:

(1) Henrietta Amalia von Anhalt, 1696–1707
(2) Maria Louise von Hessen-Kassel, 1711/1722–1731
(3) Anna of Hannover, 1751–1759, later Ludwig Ernst Duke of Brunswick-Wolfenbüttel, 1759–1766

Appendix II

Glossary of Dutch Military Terms

Adjudant	Adjutant.
Armée	Army.
Artillerie	Artillery.
Augmentatie	Augmentation, expansion.
Bajonet	Bayonet.
Bataljon	Battalion.
Batterij	Battery.
Brigade	Brigade.
Brigadier	Cavalry general, commanding a brigade.
Cadet, Kadet	Cadet.
Carabinier, Karabinier	Carabineer.
Cavalerie, Ruiterij	Cavalry, Horse.
Compagnie	Company.
Cornet, Kornet	Cavalry standard bearer, junior officer.
Divisie	Division.
Dragonder	Dragoon.
Duitse Regimenten	German regiments, specifically the Waldeck and Saxe-Gotha Regiments.
Escadron	Squadron.
Fuselier	Fusilier.
Garde, Guarde	Guard, i.e. '*Garde te Voet*', Foot Guards, '*Garde te Paard*', Horse Guards.
Garnizoen	Garrison.
Gedeputeerde	Representative, i.e. of the States General.
Generaal	General.
Genie	Engineers.
Geschut, Kanon	Artillery piece(s), gun, cannon.
Geweer	In general a weapon, but often used to denote a musket or rifle; i.e. '*schietgeweer*', firearm; and '*zijdgeweer*', sidearm (hanger, rapier, sword).
Granaat	Grenade.
Grenadier, Granadier	Grenadier.
Hautboist, Hoboïst	In general a musician, in particular an oboist.
Hellebaardier	Halberdier.

Huzaar	Hussar.
Ingenieur	Engineer (officer).
Inhaber	Colonel-proprietor of a regiment.
Infanterie, infanterij	Infantry.
Invaliden	Invalids.
Jager	Light infantryman, sharpshooter; German: *Jäger*, French: *Chasseur*.
Kapitein	Captain.
Kapitein-Generaal	Captain-General; commander-in-chief of the armies of the States.
Karabijn, Mousqeton	Carbine.
Kolonel	Colonel; i.e. *Kolonel-commandant,* colonel-commander.
Korporaal	Corporal.
Kwartiermeester	Quarter master
Leger	Army.
Legioen	Legion, Free Corps consisting of different troop types.
Lijfregiment	Life Guards Regiment; also '*Lijfcompagnie*', Life Guard (Colonels') company.
Luitenant	Lieutenant; also '*sous-lieutenant*', 2nd lieutenant.
Majoor	Major.
Marinier	Marine.
Meester, Grootmeester	Master, Grandmaster; titles of commanding officers of the artillery.
Militie	Lit. Militia; military, the armed forces.
Mineurs en Sappeurs	Miners and Sappers
Musket	In general a musket, in particular a matchlock musket.
Musketier	Musketeer.
Muzikant	Musician.
Nationalen	National, i.e. '*Regiment Nationalen*', National Regiment.
Onderofficier	Non-commissioned officer.
Pallas	'Pallasch', in general a cavalry sword, in particular a heavy cavalry sword.
Paukenslager, Pauker	Kettledrummer.
Peloton	Platoon.
Picqeur	Horse master.
Piek	Pike.
Piekenier	Pikeman.
Pionier	Pioneer.
Pontonniers	Pontoon troops.
Raad van State	Council of State, advisory body to the States General; members were nominated by the Provincial States and appointed by the States General.
Raadpensionaris	Grand Pensionary; comparable to a Prime Minister.
Regiment	Regiment.
Repartitie	Establishment, i.e. '*Repartitie van Holland*', Holland Establishment.
Ritmeester	Cavalry Captain.
Ruiter	Cavalryman, trooper.
Schotten	Scots, i.e. '*Regiment Schotten*', Scots Regiment.
Sergeant	Sergeant, NCO.
Schrijver	Literally 'writer', a secretary or clerk, also paymaster.
Snaphaan, Fusil	'Snaphaunce', flintlock musket.
Soldaat	Soldier, private.
Solliciteur	Paymaster.
Sponton, Partizaan	Espontoon.

Stadhouder	Stadtholder; mostly a military leader, comparable to a Lord Lieutenant.
Standaard, Vaan	Cavalry standard; a '*vaan*' in the 17th century also denoted a cavalry company.
Staten	Provincial parliament, i.e. '*Staten van Holland*', States of Holland.
Staten-Generaal	States General; parliament of the Dutch Republic with representatives of all the provinces and counties.
Tamboers en Pijpers	Drummers and Fifers.
Timmerman	Carpenter, infantry sapper (plural: '*Timmerlieden*').
Trompetter	Trumpeter.
Vaandel, Vendel	Infantry colour; in the 17th century also used to denote an infantry company.
Vaandrig, Vendrig	Ensign.
Wachtmeester	Cavalry NCO.
Walen	Walloon, i.e. '*Regiment Walen*', Walloon Regiment.
Waterlinie	'Water Line', a large area that was flooded to halt invading troops; the main line of defence against invaders during the 17th to 20th centuries.
Vrij Compagnie	Free Company, irregular troops.
Zwitsers, Switsers	Swiss, i.e. '*Regiment Zwitsers*', Swiss Regiment.

Appendix III

Glossary of Dutch names for French and English Toponyms

Aat	Ath
Aken	Aix-la-Chapelle
Antwerpen	Antwerp
Bergen	Mons
Brugge	Bruges
Brussel	Brussels
Dijle	Dyle
Doornik	Tournai
Duinkerke, Duinkerken	Dunkerque, Dunkirk
Gent	Ghent
's-Gravenhage, Den Haag	La Haye, The Hague
Henegouwen	Hainaut
's-Hertogenbosch, Den Bosch	Bois-le-Duc
Luik	Liège
Kamerijk	Cambrai
Kortrijk	Courtrai
Maas	Meuse
Menen, Meenen	Menin
Nieuwpoort	Nieuport
Oostende	Ostend
Oudenaarde	Oudenarde
Rijn	Rhine
Roer	Rur
Schelde	Scheldt
Tongeren	Tongres

Colour Plate Commentaries

Plate 1: Artillery, 1730–1772
A. Officer, 1735
Officers wore red waistcoats, breeches and stockings, unlike the rank and file, which had dark blue smallclothes. Officers and NCOs were still armed with spontoons and halberds until the 1740s. After contemporary images.

B. Gunner, 1745

C. Gunner, 1753
After a print, published after the reorganization of 1752, with the uniforms of all regiments in the States Army.

D. Officer in parade dress, 1769
Contrary to regulations, artillery officers had a parade uniform, decorated with gold lace; their hats had scalloped gold lace. Fusils and belly boxes for officers and NCOs were discontinued after 1774.

Plate 2: Specialist troops, 1745–1772
A. Extra-Ordinaris Engineer, 1745
After a portrait of Ernst Willem Berg; the portrait is of 1751 but the uniform remained unchanged until 1769, and it is what he would have worn when he was appointed Extra-Ordinaris Engineer in 1742.

B. Sapper, 1753
After the uniform print of 1753. Breeches are depicted here as red, as the artillery; other sources (not contemporary) give these as white or buff.

C. Sapper, 1769
The colour combination of dark blue and black with brass buttons would remain the same for the Sappers and Miners throughout the 18th and 19th centuries. After the illustration in the *Jassenboekje*.

D. Pontonnier, 1769
Uniform based on the *Jassenboekje*.

Plate 3: Cavalry During the War of the Austrian Succession
A. Trumpeter, Regiment Schack, 1739
Based on a receipt for broadcloth, buttons, and lace of that year.

B. Trumpeter, Regiment Hessen-Phillipsthal, 1743
Based on contemporary images and descriptions. The trumpet banner is speculative.

C. Officer, Regiment Van Reede Ginkel, 1740
Based on the portrait of Colonel Van Reede Ginkel. The reconstruction of the saddle housing (C1) and holster cover (C2) are based on a posthumous equestrian portrait, dated 1740, of Johan Hendrik Isendoorn à Blois

D. Trooper, Regiment Van Haersolte, 1740
Based on a schematic order of battle of 1743, and other contemporary images.

Plate 4: Cavalry, 1748–1765
A. Carabineer, Regiment Karabiniers, 1748
Based on the drawing in the *Jassenboekje;* the schematic order of battle of 1743 shows the uniform as white with red.

B. NCO, Regiment Buys, 1748
Based on a receipt of that year. The coat had white lace loops, while the buff waistcoat had buff lace loops, thus making the lace loops more practical than decorative. The receipt also mentions finer cloth for uniforms and broad silver lace for the housing and holster covers for NCOs.

C. Trooper, Regiment Hop, 1753.
After the uniform print of 1753.

D. Trooper, Regiment Van der Beke, 1764
After the *Jassenboekje.*

Plate 5: Cavalry after 1766
A. Trumpeter, Regiment Van Eck van Nergena, 1771
From the equestrian portrait of General Van Tuyll van Serooskerke by P.T. Haag.

B. Trooper, Regiment Stavenisse-Pous, 1770
As a regimental peculiarity, the coat, lined red with red cuffs, had a buff collar and buff false turned up cuffs, mimicking a buff sleeved waistcoat. After the *Jassenboekje,* and the portrait of Colonel de Jongh.

C. Trooper, Regiment De Famars, 1771

D. Carabineer, Regiment Karabiniers, 1771
Both illustrations based on the *Jassenboekje.*

Plate 6: Dragoons, 1730–1772

A. Grenadier, Regiment Schlippenbach, 1731

The grenadier company was raised in 1711, but was disbanded in 1741. The company wore embroidered grenadier caps, but their design is speculative: on the front was probably embroidered the coat of arms of Holland, as shown here; after 1737, it may have been the coat of arms of the new *inhaber* Schlippenbach, as shown on the right. The company was mounted on black horses.

B. Dragoon, Saxe-Gotha Dragoons, 1747

The unit was part of the Saxe-Gotha troops, in service of the Dutch Republic. After the war, the units were dismissed and sent back to the principality.

C. Dragoon, Regiment Trips de Berg, 1763

D. Dragoon, Regiment Hessen-Kassel, 1769

Based on the *Jassenboekje.* The Hessen-Kassel dragoon wears the plume, introduced for the cavalry in 1766. In 1769, the colour for the collar, cuffs and lapels changed to yellow.

Bibliography

Contemporary Regulations

Recueil des Ordonnances Militaires de Sa Majesté Brittanique et des Seigneurs Etats Generaux des Provinces-Unies des Païs-Bas, pour le Reglement des Troupes qui sont au Service de Leurs Hautes Puissances. Seconde Edition (The Hague: Paul Scheltus, Imprimeur Ordinaire de Leurs Hautes Puissances et Henri van Bulderen, Marchand Libraire, dans Le Pooten, 1708).

Reglementen voor de Militie van den Staat der Vereenighde Nederlanden (The Hague: Paulus Scheltus, ordinaris Drucker van de Edele Mog. Heeren Raaden van Staate der Vereenighde Nederlanden, 1728).

Recueil van Verscheidene Placaaten, Ordonantien, Resolutien, Instructien, Ordres en Lysten, &c. Betreffende de saaken van OORLOG, soo te Waater als te Lande, Part IV (The Hague: Jacobus Scheltus, 's Lands Drukker, 1749).

Reglement op de Manuale Exercitien en Evolutien van de Cavallerie en Dragonders te Paard (The Hague: Jacobus en Herman Scheltus, ordinaris dukkers van Zijne Hoogheid, 1754).

Reglement op de Manuale Exercitien en Evolutien van de Cavallerie en Dragonders van den Staat (The Hague: Isaag Scheltus, ordinaris Drukker van Zyne Hoogheid, 1769).

Archival Sources

Bibliothèque Nationale de France, département Estampes et photographie, PET FOL-ID-41, 'Les Triomphes de Louis 14, dit Le Grand, Roy de France & de Navarre, Representés par les Drapeaux, Guidons et Etandards qui ont été pris sur les Ennemis de Sa Majesté, dans les batailles, et recontres, et prises de villes, et qui ont été apportes en ceremonie dans l'Eglise de Notre Dame de Paris depuis 1674 jusqu'à la fin de son Régne'.

Bibliothèque Nationale de France, département Estampes et photographie, FOL-ID-46, 'Les Triomphes de Louis Quinze, Roy de France & de Navarre'.

National Archive, Council of State nr. 1.01.19 entry nr. 1899, journal of Pieter Johan van As regarding the campaigns of 1743, 1744, 1745 and 1747.

National Army Museum, Soesterberg, 'Overzicht der Nederlandse huzarenuniformen in 29 gekleurde platen', manuscript by A.C. Baron Snoukaert van Schauburg.

Utrechts Archief, archive of Huis Zuilen, from the papers of D.J. van Tuyll van Serooskerken, nr. 2.3.15.02 entry nr. 1015, Journal of Isaac Cronström regarding the siege of Bergen op Zoom, manuscript dated 1748.

Published Sources

Anon, *An Authentic Journal of the Remarkable and Bloody Siege of Bergen-op-zoom, By the French, under M. de Lowendahl. Begun July 14, and ended Sept. 16, N.S. 1747 […]. By an English*

Volunteer, Late of the Garrison at Bergen-op-Zoom (London: Printed for the Proprietors; and Sold by R. Griffiths, Publisher, at the Dunciad in Ludgate-Street, 1747).

Anon., *Beknopte Historie van t Vaderland, van de vroegste tijden af tot aan het jaar 1767*, part 3 (Amsterdam: Petrus Conradi, 1787).

Anon, *Nederlandsch Gedenkboek of Europische Mercurius, berigtende De Gesteltenissen der Zaaken van Staat en Oorlog, in alle Heerschappijen en Landschappen van Europa, beneevens d'aangrenzende gewesten*, several volumes:

Part 2 of the 58th edition (Amsterdam: B. v. Gerrevink en Erven Ratelband, 1747).

Part 1 of the 61st edition (The Hague: Fredric Henric Scheurleer, 1750).

Part 1 of the 63rd edition (The Hague: Fredric Henric Scheurleer, 1752).

Part 2 of the 63rd edition (The Hague: Fredric Henric Scheurleer, 1752).

Bedford, John Russel, Duke of, *Correspondence of John, Fourth Duke of Bedford: selected from the originals at Woburn Abbey* (London: Longman, Brown, Green and Longmans, 1842).

Bosscha, J., *Neêrlands Heldendaden te Land, van de vroegste tijden af tot in onze dagen* Part 2 (Leeuwarden: G.T.N. Sturingar, 1838)

Daenen, J.S.M., Th.R. Kraus and J.H.V. Notermans, *Thans bonst het grof geschut... De verovering en bezetting van Maastricht in 1748* (Maastricht: Stichting Historische Reeks Maastricht, 2001)

Dekkers, R.M. (ed.), G.J. Johannes and L.C. van de Pol, *De Bredasche Heldinne* (Hilversum: Verloren B.V., 1988).

Dibbetz, Johan, *Het Groot Militair Woordenboek* (The Hague, Jacobus van den Kieboom, 1740).

Enthoven, V. (ed.), H. den Heijer and H. Jordaan, *Geweld in de West. Een militaire geschiedenis van de Nederlandse Atlantische wereld, 1600–1800* (Leiden/Boston: Brill, 2013).

Ferguson, James (ed.), *Papers illustrating the History of the Scots Brigade in the Service of the United Netherlands 1572 – 1782*, Volume II (Edinburgh: Scottish History Society, 1899).

Forbes-Wels, F., *De Nederlandse Cavalerie* (Bussum, Van Dishoeck Uitgevers, 1963).

Hartsinck, J.J., *Beschrijving van Guiana, of de Wilde Kust in Zuid-America*, Part 1 (Amsterdam: Gerrit Tielenburg, 1770)

Haverkamp, J., *Staatsgeheimen van Europa. Naar echte Stukken en Handschriften van Staatkundige Liefhebbers, in 't Nederduitsch geschreven*, part XIX (Amsterdam: Jan 't Lam, Boekverkoper, bezuiden 't Stadhuis, 1748).

Hoof, Joep van (ed.), *Nederlandse Militaire Uniformen, 1752–1800* (The Hague: Netherlands Institute for Military History, and Vienna:Verlag Militaria, 2011).

Hey Jacobsz, J. van der, *Eerzuil, opgericht ter Onsterfelyke Gedagtenisse van Neerlands Hooge Magten wegend de Gehouden Onzydigheid, in den Jongst Geëindigden Oorlog* (Amsterdam: By de Erven van F. Houttuyn, 1766).

Kersteman, Franciscus Lievens, *Den Oorlogszwerver of Het Leven van den Grave van Tottleben. Eertyds Kollonel in dienst van de Staten Generaal der Verenigde Nederlanden, en laatst Lt. Generaal van de legers van Hare Rus. Keyz. Maj.* (Zaltbommel: By Johannes Will. Kanneman, 1761).

Kuypers, F.H.W., *Geschiedenis van de Nederlandsche Artillerie van de vroegste tijd tot op heden* Part III (Nijmegen: Adolf Blomhert, 1872).

Leune, J.G.M., *Pieter de la Rocque (1679–1760) en de capitulatie van Hulst in 1747* (Broek: op Langedijk, Gigaboek, 2014).

Nimwegen, Dr. Olaf van, *Dien Fatalen Dag, Het beleg van Bergen op Zoom 1747* (Bergen op Zoom: Sector Archiefzaken Bergen op Zoom, in Cooperation with Van der Kreek and Quist, 1997).

Nimwegen, Dr. Olaf van, *De Nederlandse Burgeroorlog (1748–1815)* (Amsterdam: Bert Bakker/ Prometheus, 2017).

Nimwegen, Dr. Olaf van, *De Republiek der Verenigde Nederlanden als Grote Mogendheid – Buitenlandse politiek en oorlogvoering in de eerste helft van de achttiende eeuw en in het bijzonder tijdens de Oostenrijkse Successieoorlog (1740 – 1748)* (Amsterdam: De Bataafsche Leeuw, 2002).

Northumberland, Elizabeth Seymour Percy, Duchess of, *A Short Tour made in the year One Thousand Seven Hundred and Seventy One* (London: Unknown Publisher, 1775).

Oebschelwitz, L.F.M. von, *Militair Handboek voor de Cavallery, of Beknopt Tractaat over derzelver Oirsprong, Voortgang, Inrechting, Wapenrusting, Exercitien en Evolutien, zoo te Paart als te Voet, en alles wat betrekkelyk is tot derzelve eigentlyke Verrichtingen, den ganschen Dienst te Veld, gelyk hedendaags, bij de welgeregeldste Legers waargenomen wordt* (The Hague: Pieter van Os, 1761).

Oebschelwitz, L.F.M. von, *Hedendaagsche Krygshandel van de Infantery; of Korte Verhandeling over derzelver Samenstelling, Wapenrusting, Exercitien, Evolutien en Manoeuvres'; Betrekkelyk tot alle derzelver eigentlyke Verrichtingen en gantschen Dienst te Velde, Gelyk hedendaags, bij de Welgeregeldste Legers waargenomen wordt* (The Hague: Pieter Gerard van Balen, Boek-, Konst- en Kaartverkoper in de Spuystraat, 1761).

Smits, Marjan, and Vogel, Hans (eds.), *Een oorlogsman van dezen tijd en beminnaar der sexe – De autobiografie van Casimir graaf von Schlippenbach (1682–1755)* (Amsterdam: Uitgeverij Augustus, 2007).

Whitworth, Rex (ed.), *Gunner at Large. The Diary of James Wood R.A. 1746–1765* (London: Leo Cooper, 1988).

Magazine and Journal Articles

Carter, A.C., 'The Dutch as Neutrals in the Seven Years' War', in 'The International and Comparative Law Quarterly', volume 12, nr. 3 (July)

Nimwegen, Dr. O. van, 'Van vuurkracht naar stootkracht en vice versa. Veranderingen in de bewapening van het Staatse leger tijdens de Spaanse Successieoorlog (1702 – 1712)', *Armanentaria* 30 (1995).

Nimwegen, Dr. O. van, 'Kanonnen en Houwitsers. De Staatse veldartillerie in de eerste helft van de 18e eeuw', *Armanentaria* 3 (1997).

Pijnen, F., 'Putte en de Oorlogsperikelen A. D. 1747', *Tijding - Kroniek van de heemkundekring 't Zuiderkwartier* (1985).

Sloos, Ph., 'Eendracht bij Leger en Vloot', *Armamentaria* 43 (2009).

Wilde, F.G. de, 'De Kledingvoorziening in het Staatsche Leger', *Armamentaria* 21 (1986).

Wilde, F.G. de, 'Onderscheidingstekenen voor de officieren en onderofficieren in het Staatse Leger tot 1795', *Armamentaria* 25 (1991).

Wilde, F.G. de, 'De uniformering van de Tète de Colonne 1700 - 1813', *Armamentaria* 28 (1994).

Online sources

'Dutch regiments' at http://soldaten.16mb.com/dutreg.htm

'Nederlands Militair Erfgoed' at http://www.nederlandsmilitairerfgoed.nl/nl/